Tim Hay

DARK CLOUD

No Matter How Dark The Clouds Are In Life
There Is A Friend Inside The Cloud

To order additional copies of this book, contact:
Xlibris
1-888-795-4274
www.Xlibris.com
Orders@Xlibris.com

TABLE OF CONTENTS

DARK CLOUD

I have a friend named Roy, he calls me dark cloud, and he suggested that I write a book about my experiences as a missionary in Mexico.

I was praying one-day in my front yard as I normally did and I had a vision, with my eyes closed I saw a big-screen in front of me. I saw myself in front of the county courthouse preaching to the kids who were cruising on Saturday night. After the vision I asked the Lord if I really had to do that, because I certainly didn't want to. I had never preached before. Nevertheless I had to obey the Lord. So I obtained permission from the county judge to preach on the courthouse steps with a microphone. I started preaching like John the Baptist, "repent for the kingdom of heaven is at hand". Eventually I brought a guitar and the altar from church, telling people that this is where they can start their new life being born into the family of God.

MY FRONT YARD

Three years I had been preaching in two different cities, every Saturday night, and no one wanted to be saved, because they were already saved in their own mind. These were the same people that were cussing me out, throwing beer bottles at me and flicking cigarette butts at me. One actually got out of his truck, and got right in my face like he was going to beat me up, I kept right on preaching so he got back in his truck and left. My pastor and the people of the church came out to hear me preach but became angry after the first few nights because of the abuse I was getting; they didn't come anymore after that. During this time, our youth group took a survey of over a thousand people in the area, and it turned out that 98% of the people were born again and on their way to heaven, they were very sure of that. "For unto us was the Gospel preached, but the word preached did not profit them"... "For the preaching of the cross is unto them that perish foolishness"...

SENT TO MEXICO

I was praying in my front yard as a normally did. And I asked the Lord, what should I do now, I've knocked on doors, preached in the streets I've witnessed to everyone I know, yet no one seems to want you, please Lord give me a work that I can do for you, that will change people's lives. This is when the Lord told me to go to Mexico and preach to the poor. So I started looking in the bible to see what it said about that. This is what I found.

" Jesus said unto him, if thou wilt be perfect, go and sell all that you have, and give to the poor and you will have treasure in heaven, and come and follow me" "And he said unto them, go into all the world, and preach the gospel to every creature". " And how shall they believe in whom they have not heard? And how shall they hear without a preacher? And how shall they preach, except they be sent?" "Woe is unto me, if I preach not the Gospel!" My mind and heart was set to obey the Lord. I started preparing by translating almost 100 messages from English into Spanish, not knowing how to speak the language. I bought an English Spanish Bible and typed out word for word verse for verse. I tried learning Spanish from cassette tapes , I would memorize everything on the first tape and go to the next tape memorize all of it, then listen to the first tape and found that I had forgotten, almost all the words. For about two years I was preparing to go, I sold all my worldly possessions, motorcycles, three Wheelers, boats, trucks, vans, my house, my 401(k) and all the things that I thought made my life happy and secure.

THE HOUSE AND ONE OF THE CARS

I had been very content, in my life, in my job, in my church, and I had no debt, everything was good for me and I thought that selling everything would hurt like the rich man in the Bible who kept his riches and turned from God. After I had sold everything at a great loss I felt free, free from all the stuff that hindered me from serving the Lord. Sometimes we have so much stuff that we think we need, yet it has become a burden having to maintain and keep it from being stolen, so our stuff actually becomes our God.

PREPERATION

During these two years of preparation I would pray in my yard daily. One day while I was kneeled in prayer a bird landed on my back and hopped around, I thought that was very strange yet a few days later while I was kneeled down a bird landed on my head. I was telling a friend that the Lord told me to go to Mexico to preach. And she said there's plenty of Mexicans here, why don't you preach to them. No. I said; I'm sure that I have been sent to Mexico. While I was speaking with her I told her about the birds that had landed on me, and she said; if another bird lands on you see which way it flies. I said; two birds in one lifetime are more than anyone could ever imagine, I don't think a bird will ever land on me again. The next day, I was sitting in the van that I was preparing for the first trip to Mexico, the door was open and my foot was sticking out, a bird landed on my foot for just a second, and then flew south. When I told this to my friend, she was convinced that I should go to Mexico. I was already sure.

FIRST TRIP

I took a vacation from my work as a mechanic at Tyson foods to make my first trip to Mexico; I had planned to spend this vacation in prayer and fasting with the Lord, and bring Bibles and food to poor people in Mexico, and also to find where he wanted me to preach. I got the van ready to go fixing all that needed repairing, that cost $1400. Now I was sure to have a trouble free trip. So I left very excited about the trip. A few hundred miles down the road, I had to hit the brakes really fast, and the motorcycle slipped off the front of the van and dragged under until I got it stopped, steam was blowing out from the radiator. I put the bike back on and drove to the nearest station to check it out, filled it up and found no leak, I thanked the Lord and stopped for the first night. because it was cold I lit a little gas stove for heat, I woke up in the middle of the night with my blankets on fire, and I burnt my hand putting it out. I knew that I had some engine blow by when I left but now it was getting worse, the van was getting full of exhaust smoke. It was dark now and I turned on the light inside and saw that the oil was flowing into the van from under the engine cover, about that time I heard ting ting ping ping clank clank. I pulled over to check the oil but the dipstick was covered with oil because of the oil that had been blowing out of the dipstick, so I couldn't tell how much oil was in the engine. I just poured in a gallon, and that seemed to run better. I was almost to Houston when I decided that the van would not make it, so I parked the van and rented a car. I drove to Mexico and got special insurance for the car and found out that rental cars cannot go past 25 miles into Mexico. I wanted to go further south than that, but I went anyway, looking for a small needy town. I got lost for about an hour and found the border again, then I was treated like a criminal and was picked out of hundreds of cars to be searched and questioned. They let me go, thank God. I went to return the car and found that I was two hours after the turn in time, so I had another day to drive it. I decided to go west on the border, not so crowded. I was running out of rental time and started to turn around and got stuck in a very remote place, I had to hike to the road to get help. I got help in time to turn the car back in, it was a 1500 mile trip in the rental car. I got back to the van and tried to drive it home, it was overheating and running out of oil. The oil light did not work and I could not read the dipstick, so I just put in a gallon about every 50 miles. Oil was blowing out the valve cover heavily, oil and exhaust smoke filled the van continuously, and it was getting dark so I pulled over to put oil in and spilled some on exhaust manifold which burst into flames, I could not see through the smoke and yet I still had to get oil in it. In order to keep driving I made a funnel, put a hole in the top of the engine cover and ran a hose to the oil fill hole so I could put oil in while I was driving, but the oil came up the inside and outside of the hose. Then I found a longer hose and ran all the oil and exost from the fill hole out the wing window. Oil blew out this also and this was all at night and every time adding oil was a blinding experience, billows of smoke rolling out so that I could not see the hole to put the oil in, which made the smoke worse. I decided that this was all too much for me, so I prayed and found a parking place for the night. The next morning I called to price an engine replacement, it was $1800, then I called for a U-Haul truck, it was $300. I decided to go with lesser amount, he said he had one truck, I told him I would be right over. I got there in 15 minutes and found that he had just rented the last truck to someone else. So I went to the other side of town in a crippled van to find that they were all out of trucks also. I could not leave the van because of all the stuff in it and all the money I had put into it. While I was waiting for the U-Haul truck that they were going to bring from another town,

I thought that if I found the spark plug that had oil on it, I would be able to remove it and let the exhaust come out the hole instead of into the crank case. So I borrowed a socket and tried it, I started it up and there was no more blow by. So I put another 5 quarts of oil in and headed out, only 600 miles to go. I had to wear earplugs

 because the engine was so loud. Now it started overheating because of a coolant leak, I thought it was a hose, so I replaced it and drove on, that wasn't it. It was the water pump leaking out of the seal so I filled it with water every gas station until I found some stop leak . Praise God, the leak stopped

THE SMOKING VAN

The oil was not blowing out the dipstick or valve cover, but now after all that pressure, the seals of the engine were blown out and leaking badly, not as bad as before though. I stopped by Wal-Mart before they closed, got 3 gallons of oil and set out again, adding oil blindly the rest of the way home. Now this may seem like a hard time for me, full of trouble, but I feel it was like a test to see if I would be self-controlled. I felt like it was a sort of boot camp, and confidence course that I had to pass before I could be a dedicated soldier in the Lord's army. God did provide miracles all through this trouble to encourage me. And because I complained, I fasted an extra day without food or water in repentance. Complaining to me is sin! After all that the van went through, it ran better during the last 300 miles than the first, how is that? It is God's doing. All I did was screw pipe into the spark plug hole and ran a little exhaust pipe out the back. I thank Jesus for this trying experience, it helped me to see what is really important in life, that is a relationship with him, not to be overwhelmed by external circumstances but to trust in him who is over all things. I hope that I passed the test Lord and am ready now to be a soldier in your army doing battle with the enemy. The devil! Little did I know this was just the beginning of my troubles.

SECOND TRIP

Upon my return I quit my good job of 10 years, got the van fixed up and headed out again. Driving through the deserts of southern Texas I was looking for an entrance to old Mexico, I couldn't find an entrance and asked around, this one man said there was no entrance here, but he gave me a map of the dirt roads just across the border. I found by looking at that map, to get there I would have to go in at Eagle Pass, Texas. I went into Mexico at the Eagle Pass bridge, after about 25 miles I was stopped by the federal police. I couldn't understand what they were saying, but they could speak some broken English and told me that I needed a permit for my vehicle and a visa for myself to go any further into Mexico. I went into the office and started the process, it was difficult because I didn't know Spanish, but they knew a little English also. I got the visa and was on my way. It turned out that I had to go south, in order to go west, in order to go north, in order to go west, in order go south. I was driving for what seemed like forever and this was my first trip into the interior of Mexico. I had been driving a long time when the paved roads finally ran out I never realized how much dirt and dust could come into a vehicle. I was covered with dust and breathing it. Finally, I arrived at the little town that was on the map. I drove through and found that the people were looking at me very strangely as if they had never seen a white man. I just kept driving through until I came back to the main road. I wanted to see the huge lake that was on the map. I drove south for about 15 miles on a very bad road and found that the lake was completely dried up. It was huge, as far as the eye could see, there was even a mirage. You could land a 747 on it easily.

Dried up lake

FIVE HOURS TO THE NEAREST PAVEMENT

I drove north back to the town and found a little hill overlooking the town, got on my knees and prayed saying; Oh Lord I have been searching weeks now for where you want me to go. Please tell me where you want me to preach Lord. Because I know this cannot be the place. The Lord's strong reply was; THIS IS THE PLACE!

At this point, I was very tired and stressed and said; Lord, I will die here, there's no water. (And I almost did die, later in story) Nevertheless, I knew that I had to obey the Lord, so I got out my little Spanish dictionary and found the words; can I stay here for a few days? I had to write that down in order to remember it. I drove back into the town and found an old couple in front of their house and read what I had on the paper to them. Surprisingly they were glad to see me and offered to let me stay in my van at their house. These people robed me three times and lied about it, but I learned most of my Spanish from them. Being in a place where no one speaks English, I was forced to learn Spanish. I either learned to speak Spanish, or did not speak to anyone. Living in my van without air-conditioning was very uncomfortable. But I started my work in the Catholic Church, thinking that was the only church in the town. They were all glad that I wanted to work in the church. But I couldn't understand anything they were saying. And they couldn't understand me. One time some missionaries from the city came, they could speak English, so the elders of the town wanted to have a meeting with me to find out what I was doing there, I just told them, through the interpreter, that I wanted to stay here and serve the Lord. That seemed to be OK with them. So after couple weeks I left to get my Winnebago in Arkansas. I parked the van at the border and took a bus to Arkansas. In Abilene the bus driver let me off at the station which was closed, and said your bus will be along soon. I spent two hours waiting in the middle of the night outside and it was cold. Then I found out that the bus was only going to Little Rock and would not be able drop me off where I wanted to go, so when I got to Little Rock, I called my pastor to come get me, and he did. I got the Winnebago packed up and headed off to Mexico again. Surely I would be comfortable with a generator and an air conditioner. This time I entered Mexico through Presidio Texas, because it was not necessary to get a permit and visa there. After days of driving, I finally made it to the dirt road. It only took me 12 hours from there, the roads were very bad, about halfway through the desert I found that there was military checkpoints in various places. Their jobs were to search all your possessions for drugs or weapons, after an hour of searching they let me go, even though I couldn't speak Spanish to them. I finally made it back to the little town, La Rosita and stayed for another week or two. By the way, the air conditioner didn't work. While staying there, a man came over and asked me some questions about religion. He asked me if I was Catholic, and I said no. He asked why are you working in the Catholic Church. I said, because it's the only one, he said, no it's not. There's a little Baptist Church on the other side of town. I had been spending time with the youth of the town and some of them decided they wanted to serve the Lord, I recommended that they go to the Baptist Church. It turns out that the pastor of the Baptist Church had recently died. That was an open door for me to preach. God does know what he's doing! The man, Lucha by name, was the only man in the church, and he played the guitar for the church services. So I realized that my work for the Lord here was to help this man become the pastor of the church. Praise God, he was very willing to learn. I returned to Arkansas for supplies.

THIRD TRIP

I bought a bus with my 401K money and filled it with food, clothes, Bibles and Bible comics for the kids. I went to get the bus from Arkansas and brought it to the border, but they would not let me through with the bus or the stuff that was in it. I was stuck at the border with stuff I wanted to bring in. They turned me around

and told me I need a special permit. I spent two whole days trying to get this permit with a letter from a local church and found the office in Mexico to get it stamped, well fine, again to the border with my stamped letter and the policemen would still not allow me to go through.

THE BUS BEFORE THE TRIP

I drove the bus to a place where I knew I could bring stuff across the river in a boat, it was in big bend Park, Texas. I rented an RV spot for three days, unloaded all the stuff from the bus and left it there. I drove the bus back to Eagle Pass, and finally convinced them to let me in to Mexico with the bus empty. Now I had to take the long journey on dirt roads back to the same river I had just come from. I brought all the stuff to the river and a ranger opened the gate for me. One small boatload at a time, we brought everything across, except two barrels of gasoline, I had to float those across while swimming. All the poor people in the community were helping me, they wanted stuff too, so I left one barrel of gasoline for all of them to distribute amongst themselves. The bus was loaded, and I was on my way again. Nighttime had come, and I was almost to the little town. When the axle broke, my right front tire rolled off into the desert. I had my old motorcycle in the bus, so I took

Lucha and family 1998

it and drove all away to San Antonio, got the axle off of an old truck, headed back to Eagle Pass and checked into a hotel. At this time, I was more than exhausted; in fact, I think I was having a nervous breakdown. I stayed in the room for, I think, four days, trying to recuperate. Finally, I headed back with parts in hand to fix the bus with. When I got back to the bus, it had been vandalized and robbed, no tires, no motor or transmission, windows broken and all the stuff I wanted to give to people was gone.

THE BUS AFTER

What I had planned was to make the bus like a little store, going to each house, letting the people get what they want, each one with a certain amount, and some Bible stuff. Well, I guess some poor people got the stuff, but not the way that I had intended. That bus had a permit to be in Mexico, and there was no way I could get it back

out of Mexico. I couldn't get a police report, because there are no police in the desert, so I took a picture of what was left and brought it to the lady who gave the permit in order to prove that I couldn't get the bus out. Two years later, she finally took the bus off my record.

STUCK IN THE MUD

I had to find a way into Mexico without these inspections. A man in La Rosita told me about a way to go in and out of Mexico driving through the river. So I went out that way in order to find the entrance. After driving many hours on dirt roads, I found it! The name of it is San Vencente. I came to a part in the dirt road that it was very muddy and covered with water. I got out of the truck to investigate how to go through it and found someone else's fresh tire tracks, they were skinny little tires with no tread on them, so I decided that with my good tires I could make it through, if I just got up enough speed, so away I went, I got terribly stuck about halfway through. I got out of the truck and stepped into 2 feet of water and mud. I started digging out the mud from under the tires with my hands but it was not working very well, by this time I was getting frustrated. I had been stuck for hours, I tried using a jack to lift the tires out of the mud and put rocks in, I had to hold my breath putting the jack under, still no success. On my knees, all muddy, tired and frustrated. I asked Jesus. Please help me! A few minutes later, three men on horses showed up and asked if I needed help. Thank you Jesus! They tied off with ropes to my bumper. One rope broke, but they kept trying as I was revving the engine, I finally got unstuck, I found out later that the tire tracks that I saw were from horse-drawn wagons. So me and my truck were completely drenched and muddy, I made it to the US. I started back to Eagle Pass and realized immediately when I got on the paved roads that the truck was not accelerating. I tried a few things, checking the fuel filter and lines and found that the fuel pump was bad. The reason I didn't notice it on the dirt roads was because my average speed was less than 30 miles an hour. Now that I was on paved roads, 30 miles an hour was my top speed. It took me two days at 30 miles an hour to get to a parts store that had a pump, I installed it and the truck worked fine. I made it back to Eagle Pass, where I had a P.O. Box that I received my $400 a month, payments for the house I sold. That is how I was able to live in the desert and support myself.

I returned to La Rosita and started working in the Baptist Church. It was working out great, I preached on Wednesday night, and Lucha preached on Sunday night. We were getting along great and the church was growing, **here**even though I preached some Pentecostal messages.

The Church was growing, old fence

MY WIFE REINA

After about a year in La Rosita I would sit on the hood of my truck in the evenings and listen to the families in their adobe houses, happy sounds, I realized that I missed having a family and I was alone. I had been serving the Lord for eight years without a woman or family. I went to a little store one evening and as I was leaving a woman and her daughter came out to speak to me, she was interested in me and what I was doing in this desert. At the time I didn't speak Spanish very well but this woman was easy to talk with. As I spoke with her it grew dark, I said good night and started walking, soon I was very lost, in a place with no lights that is easy, I wandered around for about an hour before I found my way back to where I was staying in my van. After a while I was visiting her almost every day where she lived with her parents and two children, her boy was one year old and her daughter was six. She would not go with me anywhere, so our dating consisted of sitting outside in the evening watching the satellites go by, in the presence of her parents. After about six weeks of this I asked her to marry me, she said yes, but I would have to ask her father for permition, the next day I did, he only requested that I remember the whole family. We went to a civil servant in the desert and he married us, then we planned a wedding in the church. The pastor and his sister the Sunday school teacher were not married to there partners yet, so all three couples got marred at the same time. This is when I bought the adobe house that I was living at, and started fixing it up for the family. We went to the border with the marriage certificate and tried to cross, they

said that Reina needed a passport. I went to an immigration lawyer to find out how to get my family across, he said it would be $800.00 per person and about eight months. I thought it would be easier just to go get her a passport myself. We took a two day trip and got lost in Monterrey, we stayed the night in the back of the truck in the parking lot after finding the place to get the passport. We got up early just to find a line two blocks long, after waiting in line all day in the sweltering heat; they told us that we needed the birth certificates of the parents also, so we returned to get them. Five days of driving we returned and waited in line again, That afternoon they gave s a paper and told us to pay at the bank across the street, this line was only one block long, after paying we went back and they let us in the building to wait for our number to be called, we got to the window and they said that we still lacked paperwork, there we received a list of the documents needed, and told that we could get a refund at the bank, we waited in line at the bank again and they said we would have to go to a different bank for the refund. At this point I was getting frustrated. We went back and got all the stuff on the list and returned, waited in all the lines and paid again. Reina got her passport but her son had to get a doctors certificate, we spent three days getting that, and returned to stand in line and pay again. So we were off to the border again, this time they said that she needs a visa, and that we could get one in Nuevo Laredo, so we headed down there and stood in line for hours only to find out that Reina did not have her birth certificate, the people in Monterey did not return it to her. Very frustrated, I left Reina at her sister's house and went to a job in the U.S. this was becoming very costly, and with many breakdowns it covered a period of about six years. Upon returning we wanted to try again but now the passports were expired so we had to do it all again, we were experts now. After getting new passports we went back to Laredo to get the visa, we were told that it is best to hire someone to get all the paperwork in order so we did two hundred dollars, we were told that Reina had to go alone, she went and was asked questions that she did not answer correctly from being nervous I guess, she was denied the visa. After all this I know that I should have just paid the lawyer and waited. I went back to the lawyer, paid him twenty-four hundred dollars and waited. I got letters in the mail once about every other month from the U.S. Gov. wanting money to continue processing the paper work, after a year we got an appointment in Juarez across from El Paso. I brought the family to Piedras Negeras and got a hotel. I wanted to make sure all was in order with the lawyer in Eagle Pass; he said I needed my birth certificate, not just a passport. I called California to get one and sent the money, the date was near we had to leave, we called to see if a passport was good enough, it was and we left, driving all day and night. We couldn't just drive strait there like in the U.S. where there were roads; we had to go very far south to go west to go north. We arrived at 4: AM slept in the back of the truck for an hour and went to stand in line again. All the paper work was in order said the pre checker, so we went to the window, we really thought this was it and they were going to give the visa, when the lady was almost done she looked at a piece of paper that had names on it of people that had been in trouble with the law and there was one that had almost the same name and date of birth as Reina. They asked her hard questions that she didn't know how to answer, I butted in and said she only has a fourth grade education she doesn't know, then I was asked what in the world do you have in common with her if she is so ignorant? I'm in love with her, I replied, Oh, She said. Well because of these similar names we have to take her fingerprints and send them to the F.B.I. You will get a letter in six weeks. Because it was far away we decided to wait just south of there near her sister, so we took the long journey to Eagle Pass to get my camper and returned, we waited two months and no reply, we called and no reply, so we left there, I went to a job in the U.S. I spoke to the lawyer, he said he could not get through on the phone, so he sent letters, I waited and waited, a year and a half later I got a letter saying that I had missed my appointment and that because they are very busy I won't get another appointment until the passports are about to expire, so now I'm still waiting. I think I have put over twenty thousand into this, and we wonder why Mexicans come across illegally. I finally got the last letter and it had two boxes to choose. 1 Start all over again, or 2 Cancel the petition for the visa. I have not made a decision yet.

I GOT SICK

Lucha and I were working on a wall around the church property in the terrible heat and I got sick, dehydration, vomiting and diarrhea. All the time that I had been in La Rosita I was drinking water from the well, I had diarrhea from the beginning, but I thought that eventually I would get used to the water, this was not the case. Feeling very weak, I got in my truck and drove to the nearest clinic five hours away, that is being bumped around and breathing dust for five hours. I got the medicine I needed, and I bought some 5 gallon jugs of purified water and headed back to La Rosita, expecting to get well. I found I got worse, I vomited the pills up and still had diarrhea. It turns out the water that I bought was filled up with local city water and had a new seal put on it. At this point I was dying, I didn't have the strength to

drive anywhere, so I was in the bed praying, asking the Lord for help. Now in the desert, sometimes they have training doctors who have to give one year of service to the community before they can be a full-fledged doctor. While I was waiting to die, one of these doctors arrived; she stuck an i v in my arm for four days and brought me out of my sickness. Thank you Jesus!

New fence, church growing

While I had this i v in my arm, I still went to church, and preached that you should be faithful to church, and that if you can make it there, you should be there and ask for prayer for the Lord to heal, and they believed, because that's what I was doing, while I was holding that i v poll in my hand. On every trip since then, I don't hesitate to bring water. I bought two plastic barrels and filled them up at the gas station in Eagle Pass with a garden hose. The water wasn't very tasty, and had a lot of chlorine, but after almost dying, chlorine tasted good. Oh I forgot to tell you that I had tried filtering the water, boiling it, and putting chlorine in it, but it was still poison. There was this white flaky stuff in it, they call salitre, I think its magnesium.

THE HOUSE I SOLD

The payments from my house were supposed to arrive in my P.O. Box at Eagle Pass. They did not come, I called them to ask why they didn't send a check, and they said they would right away. I had planed to just get the check, cash it and go back, but now was stuck in a border town waiting for a check that I desperately needed just to buy food and gas. I was sleeping in the back my truck, waiting for the check on many occasions, sometimes it came and sometimes it didn't. After about five months of driving nine hours each way, I got a letter saying that I was being sued for $14,000. With no money I decided to go back to Arkansas and get a job while I was waiting for the court date. I got a job stacking brick for six dollars an hour; it was a very hard job. I lost weight and learned a little bit more Spanish from the guys I was working with, very hot in the summer and very cold in the winter. It seemed like forever, but the court date had finally come. I felt a little nervous because I didn't know exactly what they were suing about, it turns out they wanted all their money back and claimed that I fraudulently sold the house to them. As the lawyer continued to make me look bad in clamming that I lied. I just answered their questions honestly. They had a plumber and an electrician testify against me, that I had gone against building codes in the construction. I was praying silently that the Lord would help me, because they had so much against me, and I did not have the money. Then the judge finally made his decision, he saw right through all their lies, and decided that I did not have to pay the $14,000 and that I would get the house back. The house was sold as is, and there were no building codes in that area. Thank you Jesus! Then I went to see the house that I got back, it was completely empty and had a lot of damage. One bathroom, and one kitchen were completely removed, they even took the pool table. This house was completely furnished, when I sold it to them and some of my own homemade furniture, it was a duplex and it was a castle built with rock and logs, it took me 25 years to build it and over 100 tons of rock. So this time I decided to hire a realtor, because I sold it to them for just payments to me, without interest. The realtor came and looked at it and said he could get about 20,000. After about six months, he said he could not sell the place with existing damage and without a good access road. So I went to the bank and borrowed $5,000, I paved a road in, repaired the house, Ran new water line, and put a new electric meter in. I spoke to my realtor and told them the place is fixed up now, but that I would need an extra $5,000. He said that he could not get that much of the House. During this time, working at the brick plant, I found an add in the newspaper hiring mechanics for Arkansas nuclear one, three years of experience were needed. I called them up And they said show up tomorrow, I've been working nukes that contract outages ever since. While I was working in California, I got a call from my realtor. He said that someone found the place and fell in love with it, he was willing to pay cash, so I signed the realtor back on. The money paid off the loan of $5,000, and I received the rest, in my account. At this time life was good. I was thankful to my Lord. I had a good job. Good bank account and money in my pocket. Also I had no debt. I was on top of the world. No more problems for me! While working in California I bought a lot of stuff to give to the poor people in Mexico.

TRIP FROM CALIFORNIA

So my truck was heavily loaded, my brakes were bad, and my transmission blew out by the time I got to Escondido, smoke billowing out from under the truck but it still functioned in first gear. I made it to a transmission shop; he tore the transmission out and found that could not be repaired. So I needed a new one. While I was waiting I had him fix the breaks. About five days past. It cost about $5,000 it was raining heavily everyday. They finally finished the truck. I hopped in and headed off for Mexico. As I was driving to Arizona, the truck started running bad. I tried many things to fix it. It turned out it was a blown head gasket. I made it to a repair shop before nightfall. He said it would be a couple days before he could fix it. I wasn't feeling well and spent the night in a hotel. In the morning I felt very bad. There just happened to be a hospital across the street. I went to the emergency room, after about an hour of suffering there, they took some x-rays and found that I had double pneumonia. They pumped me full of antibiotics through an i v. After three days the doctor said I could go; he gave me medicine and told me to drink lots of fluids. So I did. The next morning I was worse than the first day that I went in. So I went back to the emergency room and waited another hour before I got help, they put me back in my room and put me back on antibiotics and the doctor came back. He seemed angry with me; I just wanted to get well. There was a time when I felt

I was not going to get well. I always thought that I would look forward to death and be with Jesus but now I was scared of dying. After three more days I felt like I was getting better but the doctor would not release me, I had to prove to him that I could walk around the hospital and not faint. The next day he released me. When I got the bill, I found that they had double charged me for everything amounting to about $20,000. I made the first three months payments in advance, because I can't send mail from Mexico.

When I came back out from Mexico to check my mail I found they had turned me over to a collection agency. They took my three-month advance payment as one payment. So in order to protect my credit rating I paid all of it with my credit card. Big mistake! I've learned through all this that, it is not money that makes life secure. One day I had everything and the next day I lost it all. There is nothing greater in this life than knowing the Lord; when I put my life in his hands, I know everything will work out. I would rather suffer and be in his will, than have all the wealth of this world and be without him. I would rather live in a shack on a rock, than a castle built on the sand. A man could have all the riches of this world, health, family, House, good job, money, toys and still be unhappy. With my God I can lose everything; As I have done, even be reduced to living in a pallet house, covered with cardboard with no job or good health, no money, and still have happiness and joy that comes from Him. We only have a short time on this earth, what we do and what we believe is what matters, because when our life ends, then we will know that it was worth at all! Well back to when they released me from the hospital. The mechanic that replaced the head gasket parked the truck in the hospital parking lot and came to my room, for his money. I got in the truck and headed down the road, I made it to the next exit on interstate and the truck overheated, steam came out everywhere, and I pulled over. I kneeled in the dirt, weak and sick and tired. Instead of complaining or asking for help from the Lord, I decided that **I will praise the Lord!** I praised Jesus and said oh lord god, all I want to do is please you. If I lose everything it means nothing to me as long as I have you, I can make it through. So now I kneel before you in this dirt just to praise you Lord. Thank you Jesus!

I brought the truck back to the mechanic; I didn't have the time or the money to fix the truck. So I asked him if I could leave it with him until next year, and then come pick it up, he said yes. The next year I came by to pick it up, I could not find a tow bar, or a trailer to rent or buy, I could not even get someone to weld me something. So I asked the mechanic, if he would buy the truck from me. He said he didn't need it so I just left it with him. I lost all that I invested in that old truck. I made it back to Arkansas and rested.

I BOUGHT A NEW TRUCK

I went to look at some new trucks, not to buy, just look. I drove a brand new 2003 Ford ¾ pickup off the lot that day; it priced 31,000, about 45,000 with interest, and warranty. So for the first time in my whole life I was very much in debt with the truck and the bill from pneumonia. Knowing that I had a good truck, I expected no more problems. I filled up two fifty gallon barrels of water with a garden hose at the gas station before crossing the border. Just sixty miles across I filled up with Mexican premium gas, the truck started cutting out, I made it to La Rosita but then had to bring some people to another town in the desert, it started getting worse, I stopped at one little town and barrowed a hacksaw and cut off the catalectic converter thinking that it might be clogged, it ran good for a while, but then got even worse, I found that stopping helped, so we stopped a lot, then I thought if I just put it in neutral and turned the key off while still rolling it would do the same thing; it did. I think the electric pump in the tank was loosing its prime from the volatile gasoline. I headed back to the U.S. and in the middle of the night it got even worse, I was on a road that I could not pull over, so I was driving one to five miles an hour hoping that no one would run into me. I finally limped across the border and made it to the ford dealer who replaced the fuel pump.

I brought my own gas, Premium, in plastic barrels to put in my new truck, still the gas was bad, and I could see water and dirt in the bottom of the barrel. Regular gas called magna would not get me even one mile down the road because the in tank fuel pump would burn up. I made a trip to Vera Cruz and it ran good until I tried to return, I went under the truck to change the fuel filter on the side of the road and burnt both of the back of my arms badly, changing the filter didn't help. When it finally died half way back I loosened the gas tank to remove the fuel pump and it fell on my chest while lying in sharp gravel with open wounds, the forty five gallon tank was three quarters full, the gauge read only one quarter before
I started, I took a bus into the next town to buy a fuel pump, I returned and installed the pump, red to red black to black wires, put it all back together and it would not start, took it back apart and found that by putting the red wire to the black and black to the red it worked, it started right up, two miles down the road it started cutting out worse than before. From turning off and on the key, my hand and arm was so sore I could not move it. It took six days at one mile an hour to make it to the border. In two years I replaced 4 fuel pumps on a brand new truck, three sets of tires, and destroyed all the ball joints. Later I realized that mixing American gas with Mexican was the problem.

PISTOL PACKING PREACHER

On my second nuclear job I accidentally brought my pistol to work, when I went into the metal detector it alarmed, I searched for what might be setting it off, I tried again and it alarmed again, so this time I took off my coat and put it on the conveyer. I walked through with out the alarm but the security guard pulled out his pistol and shouted shut the place down, the gates were locked and the area was evacuated. They threw me in the floor and hand cuffed me, they brought me to a room and questioned me for hours. I showed them my concealed weapon permit; they said that was no good in SC. They asked why I brought the pistol in; I said; you have a rule that no arms are allowed in your parking lot so I put my pistol in the pocket of my coat and left it where I'm staying, but this morning was cold and I put on my coat forgetting that it was in the pocket. Thank God one of the security guards knew me from church and spoke well of me. Finally they sent me home and said that they would call. They called my supervisor to see what to do with me; he said that he would like to keep me, so they called me and told me to come in the next day. I came in and found out that I was not in trouble, and I ended up getting the day off that I wanted. The guys bought me a ball cap that said "I DON'T DIAL 911" and lots of people signed the hat. After that they called me the pistol packing preacher. God blesses me even when I am stupid. Others who have brought pistols into nuclear plants have never worked nukes again.

THE ONE TON TRUCK

I bought a one ton truck because the ¾ ton finally died, I welded five foot high racks on it so I could haul stuff into Mexico and give it to the poor people. I welded a large gas tank on it also. On my first trip, I loaded up heavily with carpet for dirt floors, bicycles for kids, and all the clothes that could fit on top. I went back to that place I found where you could drive through the river to cross into Mexico. It was very scary because the water had risen, about halfway through, the water was coming into the cab of the truck around my feet, the current was very swift, but I made it to the other side. Driving up the bank on the other side was more difficult, I kept sliding down the bank, I wasn't stuck I just couldn't get up the bank I kept trying and trying and praying. Just a few minutes later came two men on horses; they tied off to my bumper and pulled me up the bank. Thank you Jesus! Well things were going great this trip, but going up and down hills was hard on the automatic transmission, I made it to the town and gave the stuff to the people, but the transmission had to be replaced. I made it to the closest city in eight hours of transmission failures up and down on that horrible dirt road. I found someone to replace the transmission, he put a standard in it, we found it laying in the mud neglected, it took us all day riding around in a noisy old car with no windshield in the rain looking for the parts to make it work, it lasted for a while but on the next trip from Arkansas fully loaded again the clutch plate burned up. So I pulled over and had the plate replaced. All in all it has been a pretty good truck, I think I only had about four blowouts with new tires; it was because of the rock damage from the dirt roads that I had to travel. I made four trips in this truck heavily loaded; only one trip was without trouble. The truck I had before the one ton was a three-quarter ton GMC, it was destroyed from making trips. I made 10 trips in the three-quarter ton and I can remember on e trip I had that wasn't troubled. I found myself stranded many times in the desert with brand new tires that were destroyed. It is necessary to have two spare tires to go into this desert. This is the truck that was stuck in two feet of mud, and took off on its own when the tow bar broke. (Later in story) Many times I cried out to God in this desert feeling all alone and without help, but my Lord always came to rescue me.

One average load with tow bar

THE ADOBE HOUSE

Well I bought an adobe house for $700 and fixed it up to live in, because the motor home was way too hot in the desert sun. On my next trip back to the U.S. I took the motor home with me, I tow barred the three-quarter ton truck on the back of the motor home with a truck trailer hooked to the back of the truck and headed off, when I came to this big Mountain there was not enough power to go up the hill, I crept along until it stopped, I disconnect the truck and drove to the top of the hill and then ran back down to get the motor home and drove it to the top of the hill. The motor home didn't have good brakes, so I hooked the truck to the back to the motor home to drive it down the hill. I put the truck in gear behind the motor home and dragged it down the hill so that I didn't go too fast. I made it to the paved road after about six hours and the motor home started cutting out, I checked the fuel pump; good, cleaned the fuel filter, still cutting out. After a few hours of that I

found cracks in the rubber fuel lines, they were sucking in air. I made it to the first parts store and replaced the hoses in the dark with a flashlight in my mouth with gas dripping all over me. Back on the road I got pulled over by the local police who said that I needed lights on the back of my truck and not just on the trailer that was behind that, I paid him twenty bucks and went on. I finally made it out of the desert with this long rig, and as I was going through the toll booth at the border it was a tight turn and the truck broke the arm off of the toll booth. They told me to go to the office to pay for the damage, but they told me not to leave until after the police had left because they would want to charge me also. After the police left, I went and put the arm and back on the tollgate.

As I was going through Dallas I stopped for gas and headed back to the interstate as I driving along and noticed that I had more power than usual and then I realized that the three-quarter ton truck and trailer was not hooked to the back, so very nervously I rushed to the next exit to turn around, I came back looking everywhere, it was night and I couldn't find it. I got back on the interstate looking everywhere, I couldn't find it, I rushed to the next exit again and came back and noticed there was a side road after the gas station by the on ramp, I went down that road looking in the neighborhood and found the truck with the trailer behind it smashed into a dead tree in someone's front yard, this could have been tragic I believe it had the speed go right through the house and kill somebody if they were home, but thank God it only hit a dead tree in the yard, so I started it up to hook it back up to the motor home more securely this time.

CONSTRUCTION OF PLAYGROUND

I returned with a new load of stuff for the people, the church was growing so I only gave the stuff to the faithful church people. I started working in the community, I found there community Plaza or playground had nothing in it, so I gathered up the metal that I had and built some swing sets, monkey bars, and I found some big old cable spools and made a marry go round out of one, and made a squirrel run out of the other. It was good to see people in the town square every evening now that the kids had a place to play, many of the parents went, sat and talked while they were watching them. I used the welder that I had with the generator to fix all the chairs and tables in the school, and the basketball court door, and hoops. The stuff the people brought to me was some times hard to fix like one time a guy brought me a truck that the frame was broken in half, I patched it back

together. And ball joints, I would weld them back into their sockets. I even welded brackets on the fence around the Catholic church, and everyone in the town liked me, I guess that's why they didn't get real mad and run me off when I put together a message on the Catholic religion, all I did was point out the differences between their doctrine and the bible. I typed it up and gave everyone a copy in the town, they asked why I would interfere with their doctrine, and I just told them that it was my job to get the word of God to the people.

BUILT A JAIL

The town has meetings every month, and I went for a while to see if I could help, one time they were complaining about this man that was a drunk and was being a nuisance in the town, no one knew what to do, I suggested building a jail, you can't have justice without a jail, they thought that was a great idea, and said go ahead. I thought I would be getting some help, but some kids and I used chisels to bust a door in an old rock water tank, it took eight days, and we still didn't get it all chiseled out, but it was enough to put a steel reed bar door, the jail house was ready. There were some young men, who caught robbing a house, and they were speaking about it in the meeting, my suggestion was, put them in jail until they've paid for the merchandise, or have them clean up all the trash that people have been throwing in the entrance to the town. They did not take my advice, and did nothing to the robbers. I had gone to many meetings, and had many suggestions, but they hardly ever used my ideas, they couldn't even vote on anything because all the people didn't come, I stopped going to the meetings because nothing was being accomplished there at all.

BAD WATER

I started having pain in my lower back, and I thaught that mabee I had been lifting too much, so I took it easy for a few days, later I went to make a phone call, and while walking back I fell to the ground in pain, and someone driving by picked me up out of the dirt and brought me to the house. I had to make another trip to the hospital, six hours away. When I got there he told me it was my kidneys. I thought drinking good water was all I needed. It turned out that the dirt (which is everywhere) was in my food and in the air that I was breathing, this caused me to ingest the poison that was in the dirt. When we fill the tanks up with water from the well with a bucket, and it sets awhile you can see this white stuff in the bottom, when people wash their clothes you can see the line where the water dried, it is white. On some kids you can see the same stuff on their forehead from sweat. I think this stuff is magnesium. My idea is that over the years of people dumping their wash water out on

the ground it becomes dust that is picked up by the wind and carried around.

There was these strange bugs also that would land on us in the middle of the night, they would urinate acid on the skin, it would make a blister and if you scratched it, it would spread.

Spring water from the mountian was bad also

GEORGE

One hot day I wanted to go swimming in the canal that was a few miles away, the kid next door wanted to go also, so he got permission and we left on my dirt bike. While returning, the kid, George wanted to visit the people growing crops, one of them wanted a ride back with us, three people on a dirt bike two adults and George on the back. Going slowly trough a ditch the bike's shocks went down slightly, that is when George's leg got pulled into the sprocket, this stopped the bike quickly and we fell over. George was screaming, I tried to get his leg out from in-between the tire and sprocket, his bones were bent and the meat had been ripped off from the ankle to almost the knee. I had to think quickly, I put the bike into neutral, grabbed the tire and rotated it in reverse while pulling his leg out. I could see the bone and his arteries. I put him on the bike and rushed him to his mother, we all got in my truck and sped off, I was very stressed now and driving too fast, even dangerously, the mother said; slow down or we will all be killed, so I did. In record breaking time we arrived at the nearest clinic, (4 hours) the meat in his open wound was drying out like jerky, and I couldn't keep the dirt out. The first doctor tried to clean the wound without anything for the pain, he was screaming. Finally they covered it up and we got into the ambulance, it was getting dark. I didn't notice that the driver was going very slowly until a ways down the road, I asked why? he said; to save gas, I said I'll pay, drive fast! We finally arrived at a big hospital; the doctor there said they had no beds. We went to another in the city and they had no room also. We drove to another city, they looked at his leg and said that it would have to be removed, and they could not do that there. I was praying to the Lord the whole time begging the Lord to help us. Back in the ambulance on to another city, this hospital had beds but no emergency doctors on duty, it was three o clock AM. On to another city, it seemed like forever waiting to arrive. Finally at 6 AM we found an emergency doctor on duty. Now that George was in good care I had to find some money, so I left. I sold the motorcycle and the van to pay for the medical bills and medicine, and give money to the mother. Sleeping in my truck in front of the hospital waiting for news, the mother lied to me, to put me in fear. She said that I would be put in jail for child abuse and not paying doctor bills. I was really scared and stressed, I was in a place far away, that I did not know, a gringo out of place. I prayed. The next day I met a Christian man named Pedro in front of the hospital, And I asked him about all this, he said he would check it out. He came out of the office and said everything is fine. Thank you Jesus! The doctor did a great job, he stretched the muscle and skin all the way back up to its place, and he could walk fine Thank God! Back to La Rosita, the mother lied about everything, saying that I didn't pay the bills, medicine or her. Well things got back to normal, thank God.

While I was away in the city the boy friend of George's mother broke into my house and stole my new stereo and bicycle. This mans name was Jaime, I thought he was my friend, we went fishing together almost every weekend. It turned out that many times when I had left town he was the one that stole from me, now I try to be humble, but when he started whistling and laughing at my wife when I wasn't around was too much, I was going to hurt the man. It turned out that he went to the city, got arrested and went to jail. Thank God I didn't hurt him. Mexican jail is much worse than a black eye! So I have learned that if I let God judge things it is better for me, and his revenge is worse!

WORK ON THE CHURCH

In the summer time the church would be very hot, because it had a tin roof, so I bought a generator and a swamp cooler, and put them in, I brought an amplifier and guitar; I also put lights in. In the winter it was very cold in church, so I built a wood stove to keep it warm. I did not want anyone to have an excuse not to go to church, yet some people would prefer to sit in there hot adobe house suffering from heat and boredom. I would come by and invite them, and it was like; let me think, good music and air conditioning. No!

LA ROSITA

La Rosita is a town of about 450 adults and 400 children, five hours to the nearest pavement, and further than that to a city with electricity. They all live in adobe houses, normally two rooms, kitchen and bedroom. The average family is five people, some have nine. They have no running water; they get their water out of a hand dug well with a bucket, and wash their clothes outside, preferably in the shade but there is hardly no trees. They have a phone in the town, it is a twelve volt satellite phone with a dish mounted on top of the adobe house. It is operated by a car battery that is charged by a solar panel; many times I had to take the battery out of my truck to make a call because their battery was dead. The dirt in the town is insane; every morning there is a fresh coat of dust on the ground like snow just to remind me of what I was breathing yesterday. People die here a lot because doctors and medicine are so far away. When they die the people build a box, put them in it and put it in the back of a truck, everyone walks behind the truck to the grave yard across the dirt road, they dig a hole and bury them. I thought a couple times that I was next. At least it's free! Years ago the Mexican mafia grew marijuana here because of the canal and remote location, also cheap labor; drying, separating and bagging it. I know many older folks that did this; they say they never tried it. In the heat of the summer they need to hide from the sun in the adobe houses with dirt roofs. Adobe construction; they put beams or whatever they can find across the adobe bricks. One guy used truck frames. They put bamboo or yucca sticks that grow in the desert across the beams and put cardboard over that, then they pile the dirt on. When it rains once or twice a year they have to replace the dirt on the roof. In the day they hide inside from the intense sun but at night the house is extremely hot, so they all sleep outside under the stars. It is so beautiful at night watching the satellites go by. I remember suffering all day from the heat just praying for the night to come, and when it did, I enjoyed it

for about five minutes and fell asleep from such hard days of suffering in the heat. During the day I would fill up this old water tank for the kids and me to cool off. It is so dry there that after you get out of the water you have to run for cover because of how cold you are, so most of the time I just splashed water on myself to keep cool.

Sometimes you can buy fresh meat there; someone kills a cow, cuts it up, throws it over the side of their truck and goes door to door selling it. If you want to buy some, just tell them how much, and they will cut it off with an old rusty saw, throw it on a scale full of flies and it's all yours. I have been invited many times to eat with people, when I get there the table is covered with flies, and they have a little piece of cardboard with poison on it setting at the end of the table, so most of the flies are squirming around dying in your food. The flies come strait from the out house that is about forty feet away, which is about thirty feet away from the well. I bought a presto pressure cooker for my mother in law to cook her beans, because she was wasting firewood to cook. A few day later I came buy and found that she was still using that old rusted pot with holes in the lid, I asked her why aren't you using the new pot? She said that she did not want to ruin it. I asked her; if I buy you another one will you use it? She said yes. This is the mentality of poor people, making things last as long as possible. She now cooks her beans in less than half the time and fire wood.

BAD NEIGHBOURS

The man that lives up stream from me blames me for his house flooding during the rain. We are both in a dry creek bed that flows through the middle of town. One time when it was raining really hard, I went to look at the flooding, there was a lot of water backed up at my property because of the sticks and debris brought by the water hitting the fence. When I was looking over his fence he came to the window and said; see how my house is flooding? I said yes look at the water it is coming from the other side of your house not from my side. At this he got very angry and hollered obscenities at me. So the next day I started digging out dirt from my land, I took a truck load to his house and asked him if he wanted it. Yes he said. Put it on the back side of my house. I brought more than ten truck loads, after that he was content. Also in this town everybody knows what everybody else is doing. If they made a soap opera about this place it would do very well on trash TV. Many people hating each other for years about nothing.

CANDELIA

Lucha, the man that I was helping to be the pastor, was missing church a lot, because of his job, Candelia. Candelia grows in the desert like a clump of waxy green sticks about 8 to 12 inches long. They take this plant, pull it up by the roots and pack it on a truck just right in order to get as much on as possible, usually just above the cab. They bring it back to town to the boil pits they have built, there is about nine or ten in town. The pits are a hole dug underneath of a rectangular water tank, they fill the tank with water, then light a fire underneath with the old dry Candelia from previous trips, as the water boils they add acid, then pack as much green Candelia in as possible, they have racks and bars to do this, it has to be pushed below the surface

Dry on the left green on the right

of the water in order to scoop the wax off the top, they put it in buckets, let it cool and sell it to a company that comes from the city. I went with Lucha on one of these trips. We set out at about 4: AM and drove to a mountain far away on terrible dirt roads, finally at the base of the mountain we left the dirt road driving up a dry creek, only got stuck three times, I don't know how he found the stuff, anyway we got as close as we could to the Candelia, about 200 yards, he would pull it out of the ground and I carried it to the truck. About mid day the heat was unbearable so in order to get out of there sooner I started working even harder. After we thought we had a full load we started loading it on the truck, I threw it up to him with a pitch fork. Finally ready to go, it was getting dark, and a tire went flat, we repaired it in the dark and were on our way, we arrived and dumped the stuff at the boil pit. I made $20.00 for a hard 16 hour day, that is good pay for them! I decided not to do it any more. I could wash dishes for more than that in the U.S.

TOWN STORE

There came a job opening in the town store, to operate it. I prayed that Lucha would get it so he would be around more often and be able to go to church. All the town people got together to vote about it, from about twenty candidates Lucha was voted in. Thank God. The person who runs the store gets a small percentage of the profits. They sell basic commodities there like beans and flower, many times the delivery truck does not come and the store is empty. Lucha is operating the store better than anyone else before him, and he is not missing church services. Lucha sells gas also, he fills barrels in the city with his truck and sells it in town, all the rusty gas you want for $3.50 a gallon.

Alfalfa is about the only other source of income there, they plow the ground with

mules, plant seed by hand, water from the canal, cut it with a cycle, pack it in wood boxes, and the kids jump on it to pack it in, then they wrap wires around it. Each bail gets about three dollars.

Alfalfa from packaging boxes

WORK IN THE CHURCH

I bought about fifty animated Spanish bible videos, good quality, and was showing them at church every night, I invited every one every day, at first only a few came, but after rumor got around the church was filling up, standing room only. About that time the passion of Christ came out, I got a Spanish version of it, and set up the basketball court with all the pews from the Catholic Church and the Baptist church. I hooked a microphone in so that I could narrate, they all were very attentive and seemed to

enjoy it, but when it was over the people ran out not wanting to hear anything about an invitation to be born again.

I had been preaching about the Holy Ghost and the speaking in tongues at church for quite some time, the people received the message and came to the alter many times to receive this power. They had heard of other churches in the city that

spoke with other tongues. When they came to the alter I would pray for them in Spanish and in tongues, but none of them ever spoke in tongues. I prayed every day for a year that the Lord would help me to teach about this, when a Pentecostal lady moved into town.

ELISIBETH ON THE RIGHT

Elisabeth was the example of the standard of living that I was preaching, and she had the gift of speaking in tongues. Thank you Jesus? One day at church after the preaching every one was praying in their own place when another lady that I had recently been baptized fell onto the concrete floor very hard, every one heard it, then she started speaking in tongues very loudly, and she would not quit, I told the people to leave her alone but they kept standing her up, she would stand praying then fall down again. I didn't know it at the time, but this scared the people of the church, some said it was the devil, the pastor said that we should not speak in to **to**ngues in the church. This was what we were all praying for, and now that it was here no one wanted it. This was talked about all through the town, we were on the verge of seeing the power of God do great works, like miracles and healings, but instead the people

rejected this. I spoke to the pastor many times trying to show him that this is how they did it in the bible, he completely rejected it.

I BABTIZED ALL WHO WERE WILLING

I also asked him why the people that had repented in the church were not being baptized. He said; that they should prove themselves first. I said; in the bible they were baptized immediately in the name of the Lord. So I started baptizing the people, over twelve people, thank God

Cooling of on a hot day

I built an outhouse for the church

OMEDO

There was a little man in La Rosita named Omedo he threatened the visiting doctor with a gun and hit him with it, because he said that he made inappropriate gestures toward his brother's girlfriend. I believe this was false. Now the doctors don't come any more. The people would not allow the sheriff to put him in jail because he was related to the mayor of the town. A few weeks later I went inviting people to church and found a woman badly beaten with a board, a two foot 2x2, she was lying in her dirt floor bleeding badly, I could see her skull in one spot, from the wounds I could see that he hit her in the forehead first, then she put her hands on her head for protection so that the second blow smashed her finger, then he hit her on the back of the head. I put her in my truck and took the long trip to the doctor, he sewed her up and I paid him. While walking back to the truck I noticed that she was limping, we looked; he had hit her also in the leg. I brought her back home and all the people gathered around, Omedo's family also, then I got angry with them, saying that they could have prevented this by putting him in jail, they were silently guilty. Still they would not allow him to be put in jail, so the sheriff called the city police, they came three days later, and Omedo just ran out into the desert and hid until they left. One day after this they told me; there he is; I said; I will grab him and put him in jail myself, but I was persuaded not to. I was still angry that this man was free to hurt people again. A few months later Omedo stole the community generator, the sheriff called the police again. They arrived the next day and searched for Omedo but could not find him. From this time on Omedo when he got drunk would threaten the sheriff, one time because of a threat the sheriff and his family stayed at my house. About a year later Omedo got drunk went to the sheriffs' house and shot him dead! The sheriff was my father in law, I got the call yesterday, that he's dead. I loved him like my own dad.

Update, six months later I went back to Mexico and heard the rest of the story. The man Omedo was still free doing and going wherever he pleased. When I heard the story of how Omedo, being drunk and acting friendly shot my father in law in the back of the neck, and how they had to leave him lay there in the street like a dead dog until morning, when the police could there to investigate. Upon hearing this I exploded in anger and in tears of sorrow. I franticly got my motorcycle out of the truck trying to get it started to go after Omedo and "lay hands on him suddenly" My wife was frantic trying to stop me from going but I would not listen to her. Thank God the motorcycle would not run after being set up for two years, because of that I was able to calm down. I have sent money to Juan my Father in laws brother to help encourage the police to go after this criminal.

Update; Juan went after Omero with no help from the police, when he finally found him after a year of looking he was not alone; he was in the Mexican mafia. They took Juan and threatened to kill him and his family if he did not smuggle cocaine across the border. I don't know why, but he did it and got caught by the American police and now is in jail awaiting trial. Juan is a pastor in Ft. Stockton Tex. With a family of five.

MOVE TO VERA CRUZ

Because of my sickness in La Rosita from the dirt and water I prayed about leaving for two years, I was allowed to go and serve the Lord in a place where I don't get sick and there is electricity. I loaded my camper in the 2003, 250 Ford truck and hooked my fully loaded 69 Ford to the back, as we were going through the Sierra Madre Mountains we stopped for the view and billows of smoke came out from the truck, the brakes were over heated. Further down the road the tow bar broke while going down

the mountain, I stopped the rear truck by letting it hit my bumper just before coming to a tight turn that had a tall cliff. I found someone local to weld it and we continued. We arrived in Vera Cruz and bought a small piece of property.

Years later after the truck had been setting in the woods of Arkansas I needed it to make **ONE LAST TRIP** to move from the desert to a place where I wouldn't get sick, Vera Cruz I loaded up and set out, I made to the Texas line when it started getting dark so I checked the tail lights and had to fix them, when I pulled out I heard a pop, I got out, looked around and found nothing wrong, so I went on. While driving 70mph the rear

Wheels locked up, I saw smoke from the tires come up past my window, I was not able to get out of the lane, and people were blowing by me at dangerous speeds. I knew that I had to disconnect the drive shaft in order to get it off the road, so I found a little flashlight and some wrenches, finally got it loose, tied it up with a piece of rope and towed it to the next exit. The next day I took the top off of the transmission and found that it was all torn up, a guy at the tire shop said that he knew where one was so I followed him to a house where there was an old pickup in the back yard, we removed it and put it in my truck, that cost $600.00 and I was sore from turning wrenches, but I was on the road again. I noticed that I had a flat tire and pulled into a tire shop, they said that the lug nuts were rusted and could not be removed without breaking them so they got a bigger impact wrench and busted them off, the lug bolts would not be in until the next day. While I was waiting a customer who saw the problem came over and said that these old trucks sometimes have backwards treads and it turned out that was the problem. I finally made it to

Mexico and the new transmission was making terrible grinding noises but I was still moving forward, during this trip just moving forward day after day was something that I thanked the Lord for regularly. I made it to the dirt road and all the way to La Rosita, just nine hours with not much problem. I was there just four days and grew sicker every day from breathing the poisonous dust the last day I was dehydrated and not urinating just diarrhea, that is when I needed an i.v. to regain enough strength to leave the next morning a 4:AM. About one hour down the dirt road the truck stalled, it was not getting gas, I thought it was the fuel pump and how could I get a new one out here in the wilderness, looking with a flashlight I found a hole in the line from the tank and repaired it. By the time the sun came up the truck quit running, when I got out to see what it was I heard the tire hissing, I tried to put a plug in the hole but it was to late, I hade to change it, when I went to put the spare on, the rim would not fit over the rear hub, so I had to change out the front tire with the rear and put the spare on the front. The sun had come up and the heat was hot enough to faint while changing tires on a one ton truck. The truck had stalled because the fuel line coming out of the tank was pinched behind the seat; I think this was an intermittent problem for years. Moving forward was a slow hard thing, and I was very thankful for it. The truck stalled again, after checking everything it was the pump this time, what was I to do so far from anywhere? I thought that if I could just get gas to the carburetor, but how? I found a five gallon gas jug in the back of the truck, and thought if I put this on the roof with a hose to the carburetor it would siphon, I used my air compressor hose to siphon gas out of the tank, filled the jug, put it on the roof, ran the hose under the hood to the carburetor, I primed the hose, and closed the hood on a screwdriver handle in order to not pinch the hose. Praise God! It worked; I only had to stop four times to refill the jug from the gas tank. I finally made it to the pavement after six hours in the desert heat and dust. An hour later I arrived in the city, a parts store, hotel, air-conditioning and a shower.

Thank God! The next day I put on a new fuel pump, all new lines and fuel filters. Moving forward again, the noise in the transmission was getting worse when the truck stalled again, I looked at the new filters and both were filled with rust, before and after the fuel pump. I removed the filters and ran the lines direct in order to get to the next parts store. There I put two new filters in and it ran a while, but now the new pump was ruined from the rust. I stopped at parts stores but no one had the pump I needed, so I was back to the gas jug on the roof. Now the transmission noise was loud and terrible, I stopped to put in oil but it was full, the color of it was grey from all the metal in it. Moving forward, finally there were violent clanking noises, I pulled over at a gas station to ask about another transmission, there was none.

I started taking off the drive shaft again and tie it up in order to have someone tow me the rest of the way with the tow bar that I had. I found that the differential had come apart due to the first transmission lock up. I tore the differential apart, axels and all. I rode my bicycle and found bearings in the store, cleaned up the damaged splines that had been wallering around. I installed the new parts; I was very exosted and very filthy but I was getting very close so I continued. In one town I was driving through a policeman stopped me and said that I was driving in the wrong lane; cargo trucks should be in the right lane, and he had a list of other false infractions; it all came down to what they all wanted; money, but he wanted $300.00 for him and his partners, because of my white skin I know it is not worth it to argue, I gave it to him and said if I give any more I won't be able to arrive. Later that night I took a wrong turn and went into the city, a policeman stopped me and led me out of the city to the bypass road. I gladly paid him $20.00. Loosing the prime and running out of gas became a frequent problem, three times it stalled at a place where no one could pass like on a bridge where the police were watching and I am on the roof trying to prime the hose from the gas jug. Now the transmission would not shift to fourth gear, this caused the use of more gas, moving forward slowly I finally arrived. Thank God! This trip was the longest and most troublesome of all but with help from the Lord I never got angry and just moved forward as best I could.

I did learn some things in this trip; a jug of gas on the roof does work good, never drink the water in Mexico or the ice, don't even brush your teeth with it, and do not drive in Mexico! Take a taxi, bus, or plane. Not getting angry helps to accomplish a lot more. And prayer can get you through anything!

ACUNYA

Many times we went to visit my sister in law, she lived in Acuna, and her house was made of pallets covered with cardboard, one room with a bed and a little electric burner to cook on. The out house was just outside, it was on the side of the hill and it was leaning, it was a community outhouse and it was nasty, I had to use it while visiting. She came here in order to work in the American factory in town, along with many others who live in their pallet houses on the hills above the town. The approximant income is $30 per six day week, they take a bus to work and back, if they had a car they could not afford to put gas in it. They have a little black and white T.V. and a little refrigerator that I gave them. Her sister across the dirt street has a smaller block house, with there very own toilet out back. The toilet has three pallets and a blanket for the door, when your sitting on it all the neighbors can see you, and in the winter it is very cold. The toilet sets on a board over a hole in the dirt, it has no tank, and you have to fill up a bucket from the community faucet out front. Their shower is four pallets stood up against the back of the house, they heat water on the burner, bring it around the back and pour it on themselves with a cup while standing on a little rock in order to not get their feet in the mud. Having to bathe like this myself in the winter made me want to do something about it, with just a small amount of money I bought four more used pallets and made a room out of the shower area. I busted a door in the back wall where the window was to make the entrance; I wrapped it in old carpet and roofed it with plastic, now the warmth from the house was in the bathroom. I put two plastic pallets for the floor, put the toilet in, ran a sewer pipe to the old hole, I put a Y connector on the community faucet, and ran a garden hose to the room with a spray handle. Now they have indoor plumbing, heat and privacy. I woke up one morning while staying in the pallet house and some one was at the door with blankets and bibles, I came out and they asked; what are you doing here? It was very strange to them to see a white person in this area; I told them that I wanted a blanket too! I recently returned to Acuna and taught my son to swim in the sewage river called the Rio Grande.

MONCLOVA

When we were passing through a town eight hours south of La Rosita we saw lots of smog coming from the factories, it filled the town, and I wondered how the government could get by without some kind of controls. Just then we were stopped by a man that wanted to check our emissions, we had to pay for a smog sticker, I don't think his tester even worked. It turned out that the people had been complaining about the smoke from the factories, instead of fixing the problem, they put it back on the people. The Mexican Federal Government has all the power, they own Pemex, all the gas and all the electricity, they have most of the guns also, and they are illegal in Mexico.

MOTO TRIP INTO THE DESERT

I took a trip on the motorcycle in order to save the truck from being damaged from the road to La Rosita. I put water and extra gas in a bag, strapped it to the bike and left on a Honda 250 rebel street bike; it was great until I made it to the dirt part. First I lost the bag and went back for it; I put it on my back. The rear tire was hitting the fender almost every bump, the license plate broke off, then the battery fell out (held only by the cables). I put the battery back in with bunji cords. I was going fast because it was a long trip, normally five or six hours. Then the windshield came off, I left it in the desert. While I was riding I could see that the goose neck nut was loose, so I just kept it tight with my fingers, I was hitting pot holes very hard, one time I hit one so hard that the left handle grip came off in my hand, I almost lost control. Finally there was an electrical fire from wires that were pinched under the seat, I unplugged everything to stop the wires from burning, other than that it was a successful trip, Three hours.

WHERE TO PREACH

When I was looking for where in Mexico that the Lord wanted me to preach, I went to Baja California, and said "Lord this would be a great place to preach, near the ocean, he said "NO". I went to the gulf coast and said "Lord this would be a good place, he said "NO". I went to Juarez, he said "NO". Every where I went he said no until I arrived in La Rosita; it was a definite "YES" even though I did not want it.

BEFORE I MET THE LORD

POISIONED

When I was a baby they say that I ate some poison, my dad drove like a mad man, he blew through the military check point, the police were after him but he would not stop until he got me to the doctor. I was dieing in the hospital, the doctor said that I would not survive the night. All the people who knew about it were praying for me. After that I recovered with no side affects. My mom always told me that the Lord had something very special for my life. That was true!

MY FIRST LOVE JENNY

I have only been in love with three women in my life, my first love was Jenny. I

remember one day as I left to walk home, how she walked with me to the edge of the orange grove and kissed me for the very first time. The first night that I knew that I was in love, I was listening to Pink Floyd dark side of the moon on eight track so it played over and over, this became the most romantic music to me, even now when I hear it I think of Jenny. I was so in love with her that I would do all my chores on the farm and do my homework as fast as I could in order to be with her, I would run about a mile to her house every day, nothing in life was more important to me than her. I always tried to impress her, one time I took her to a dried up pond on the motorcycle that I bought from her brother, I let her off and said watch this; I spun out and did a jump out of the earth tank, when I got up in the air is when I found out that it was the dam that I jumped off of, I think it was about thirty feet in the air, it seemed like slow motion, I decided it would be best to get off the bike and I landed on the slope of the grassy dam, the motorcycle landed in a tree, I had to climb the tree to get it out. I remember the first time we made love, it was under a fig tree behind her house and we were both virgins, it was one of the most memorable moments in my life. Looking back now I see that I made a lot of mistakes, I guess that I didn't really know how to love someone. I remember one night me her and her brother Gilbert went camping, I didn't have a sleeping bag so I stayed close to the fire to keep warm. Jenny looked at me and said; do you want my sleeping bag? I wanted so much to say, only if you stay in it, but I was too shy. I took the sleeping bag while Jenny sat by the fire all night, my shyness actually made me stupid; I wanted to be in the bag with her. It is hard to believe that she fell in love with me after doing something like that. I was so in love with her but failed to protect her and be the man. One of my school mates that was bigger and stronger than me would go up and pinch her nipples right in front of me, I told him not to do that, but he continued on various occasions. I should have jumped him from behind and choked him till he fell to the ground, but I was afraid, what a wimp I was. I think that this is why she may have fell out of love with me, and started treating me accordingly. One day came and I had enough, I went to break up with her, and I asked for my ring back and for a puppy dog to take her place, she looked bewildered, I didn't explain anything, and I gave her no reason. I was still very much in love with her. I would be at a party and that music Pink Floyd would come on, I would go into a trance thinking about Jenny. I alienated good friends because of my feelings for her. I remember being at school at El Capitan thinking how wonderful it would be just to talk to her again. Even after I graduated and was in the Air Force I sent Jenny some tapes of love music but her mom said that she never opened them and that she was married. Six years after I broke up with her I still thought of Jenny. The pain of losing love is a terrible thing especially your first love. It was because of Jenny that I knew what love was, and I searched for it for the rest of my life. Even after I got married I didn't want to get rid of the pictures I had of us together. This is the only picture I have left, I think Jenny was interested in the Lord, I remember she used to watch the gospel T.V. but I wasn't interested in the Lord until I met him in the Air Force. Rod Stewart was right. **The first cut is definitely the deepest.**

BLACKOUTS

I was wild as a teenager, getting drunk on a regular basis, many times I blacked out. That is, the next day I did not remember what happened the night before. One day my friends and I went fishing at the liquor store, our girl friend asked any man entering the store if he would buy us alcohol. We got a quart of tequila and went up to the mountain to drink with lemons and salt, after we finished the first bottle, they say that we went back and got another. All I know is that I woke up all muddy and found a rope tied to the back of my truck. I had to find out what happened. They told me that we drank the other bottle and then let one of the girls drive the car, well she got it stuck. They say that I ran back to my truck in the dark and far away, came back and pulled the car out, then drove home. This was very hard to believe, because I was not there, but the evidence was. On another occasion I was at a keg party, for some reason I wanted to get my friend to follow me to his house. He had given his keys to someone else in order not to drive drunk, well I searched everywhere to find his keys; they were Alan's pocket asleep under a truck. I got the keys to him and we left, I told him I would follow him to make sure that he made it ok; about half way his car stalled under a bridge; we opened the hood and found nothing, he tried to start it again and it started, we got back in the cars and that is when I blacked out. The next day he said that he fell asleep and rolled the car, it landed on its side and he was standing on the door when he heard me drive by.

When I was in the Air Force my boss and I went to the on base bar after work, after a few pitchers of beer we left, as we stepped out the door I blacked out, next thing I was in the hospital and someone was washing my mouth out with a really stiff brush, I started hollering. After they sewed my lip back together I went to find out what happened, my boss was in the hospital also, his head was busted open, and they had to put in a metal plate. When he woke up he told me that we had a great time and he was thinking about buying a motorcycle, while we were going down the road at night he said there was a car coming at us in our lane, and that I had swerved off the road to avoid it, that is when we hit the concrete drainage pipes. My front wheel was shaped like the pipe, he was not mad at me; I thought he would be, he said that he would have done the same thing.

These are just a few of the times that I blacked out, after awhile I was wondering who is this guy, that is able to drive, speak to people, and make it home, I think he was the life of the party but it was not me and I was not there. Thank God, he was looking out for me even before I knew him.

YOUNG STORIES

When I was young I used to watch the thrill seekers on TV and after the show I would go try to do what they were doing. Once built a kite with 2x2s and a sheet, holding on to both sides of it I ran down a hill in a strong wind, I flew for a few feet but couldn't get the lift I needed.

Then I made a bike jump with boards on top of a feed card about 2 feet high, I took the jump and landed on the front tire, that's when the goose neck broke, as I landed on the ground the handlebars turned around and the gooseneck stuck me in the chest that really hurt.

One time climbing a palm tree in the front yard I was about 30 feet high and I fell, as I was falling my arm got hooked on three of the thorns sticking out of a branch,

43

I hung there being amazed that I'd wasn't dead on the ground and was able to climb back on the tree and climb down.

In my teens I was a hippie, I had the longest hair and my junior high and my high school I wore bell bottoms and dingo boots. I built a green house and enjoyed growing plants behind my fort, but was not successful in selling the plants. In junior high I would go to the bus stop and every day the bigger kids would bring scissors to cut my hair, I'd fight them off until they got tired of messing with me, sometimes they would throw rocks at me so that I couldn't get on the bus, later on they became my friends. One time on the school bus I was just sitting there minding my own business when the bus driver stopped and said that the girls had to sit on the other side of the bus, everything got quiet until she repeated saying that girls need to sit on the right side of the bus, that's when I realized she was talking to me, I got up and told her with a loud voice that I am not a girl, later I thought that I shouldn't have said anything, just went over and sat with the girls like I wanted to do. I had this old red La Bamba car that I fixed up at auto shop, I finally got it running and took it for a spin on the track around the football field, I heard later that a girl that looked like me got in trouble for it. Sometimes I would borrow my dad's pickup truck and one-time I saw snake in the road and I stopped to catch it when I turned around the truck was gone, I forgot to put the emergency brake on. I went looking for the truck and found it about half a mile away in a ditch with no damage. Once I parked that same truck at a keg party and someone else had parked his truck up the hill and his emergency brake didn't hold, it came all the way down the hill and slammed into my dad's truck, this was very hard to explain to my dad because I told him that I went to the movies in town. Another time I was smoking a cigarette with a friend behind the baseball backstop and an ex cop teacher assistant came around the corner and caught us, I slid the cigarette butt in my pocket and we were led to the principal's office, that's where they searched us and they found the butt in my pocket so they checked our records, they suspended my buddy but because I had good grades they sent me back to class.

In order to do whatever I wanted on the weekends I always told my parents that was going camping, I grabbed a few stakes from the freezer and a couple cases of beer that my dad kept in a garage, after while my dad could tell that some beer was missing so he started marking how many cases he had on a rafter so after every time I would take a case of beer I just marked it off on the rafter in the garage. I would bring beer to bus stop before going to school and got drunk before I got there. My mom had half gallon whiskey bottles under the kitchen sink; I would take a little out of each bottle and take it to my friend's house to drink straight. Later my little brother tried that but he put water to replace the whiskey and my mom knew it right away.

I started smoking pot in the third grade my older brother would give me a joint every day to take to school and smoke it with my buddy David. I don't know how but that's when my grades started improving. Much later, One night my mom asked me if she could wash my coat because it was very dirty, I said no and ran into the bedroom it was too late she found all my pot smoking stuff, papers, pipes, roach clips, and seeds, I thought my dad would punish me but instead he told me to get a hobby and quit smoking pot. He had dealt with my older brothers about this, so I guess he tried a new approach, so I started working on skates boards as a hobby, my first skate board I painted yellow and put a big pot leaf under clear enamel, I decide to take my new skateboard and ride down from the top of the hill Dunbar the paved road, speed was picking up quickly and I didn't know what to do, I thought that maybe I could go over to the side road and jump into the ice plant, then I thought that maybe I could just sit down on the state board and stop with my feet but when I tried I went into the high-speed wobbles so finally I thought that if I just jump forward running I could just run at the same speed, as I was going on skate board I tried it, I took one step and flipped onto my bare back on the pavement, it ripped the skin off my back because I had no shirt, after that skate board's were not my hobby.

One time we went on vacation to Las Vegas, I only had a couple of nickels in my pocket, as we entered into the first casino I stuck a nickel in the first machine I saw and out came about a hundred nickels, I stuck every nickel back into that same machine trying to win, when I finally found my parents who had gone ahead, they did not believe that I won and lost all that money. I never had a problem with gambling because every year at Halloween we would play poker with the candy that we got and I would always lose.

We had pigs on our farm and my dad would get old produce from the grocery store and feed it to them, me and Mark bloom got the idea to smash up the fruit and it and make our own wine. We smashed it up with our feet in a 5 gallon bucket and after about four days we poured all the liquid and put it in a bottle, after a few days we got tired of waiting for it to ferment so we drank it, we got drunk and then cooked some pizza in my Little toaster and I got terrible heart burn, the next day I found out why, there was a cigarette in the toaster oven, and I had real bad diarrhea from the fermenting wine. When I got to high school I bought a VW bug for $600, me and my party friends drove everywhere in that thing, we would buy a keg of beer and bring it to the monument at the top of Holley Rd. Once I was coming down the mountain really fast with a full carload of people, they were all screaming and pulling my hair to slow down, just then the left side of the car went off the dirt road, it was about 100 foot cliff, everyone thought we were going to die but just then I hit a rock and bounced right back on the road, I guess it just wasn't time to go yet.

On another occasion me and my little brother John were coming down the steep dirt hill at the top of Dunbar Ln. when the wire that held the brake lever broke off. With no way to stop or slow down we were picking up speed then we hit the barbed wire fence at the bottom of the hill, we both flew over, I went face first into the dirt filling my mouth with it, John landed on top of me, unhurt thank God.

MIKE

Me and one of the best friends of mine named Mike found a pond that we wanted to stock with fish but every year it would dry up, so we decided to fill the spillway in with dirt, plastic and whatever else we could find. We knew that the next rain would fill it up and that it would last all year, so when the rain came we watched it fill up. We started noticing cracks in the dirt of the dam, we thought well maybe it won't break, that very night we had a big rain. In the morning we went up to see how full it would be and to our amazement the dam was gone, it was about 30 feet from the top of the dam to where the water cut its way through and it was about 15 feet across. We went downstream to see what kind damage that whole pond of water did, it took out a lot of shrubbery and moved boulders but I don't think it did any damage to anyone's personal property. So much for our stocked fishpond.

One time we and some friends went fishing at El Capitan reservoir, it was the drinking water for the area so people were not allowed to go in there, so we snuck in

and started fishing. We were under a cliff about 25 feet down and we heard a Rangers truck pull up, we heard his door open and close, so we left our fishing poles and moved up under the cliff as far as we could to not be seen, we heard his footsteps come all the way to the edge of the cliff, just then I got a fish on my line and it started dragging my pole towards the water making noise as it went, we knew that the ranger heard it and maybe even saw the poll being dragged in, we remained quiet and scared wondering what the ranger was going to do, then we heard his footsteps, he returned to his truck and left. One day I went up Mike's house as I entered the door of his room he pointed at 12 gauge shot gun right at my face, I didn't think that was too bad until he fired it, I was probably only about 8 feet away and a piece of plastic hit me in the forehead, I was very startled. I didn't know that he could load his own shells with his dad's equipment he loaded that shell just for me, we laughed about it afterwards.

Another time I came to visit him his dog kept barking at me and would not stop, Mike said that he's all bark and no bite and that he would not bite me, so I leaned down and barked right back in the dog's face and he bit my nose, I was bleeding.

When we would get bored Mike and I would do stuff like built kites and fly them from a fishing rod and reel or build a tennis ball cannon, or just go riding motorcycles, he had a Harley 90. We would grind up seeds and stems and smoke it; it's all my brother would leave us until we started growing our own. We had a very good time in our youth.

JOE

When I was in sixth grade this big kid was picking on me, Joe came to my rescue, which is when I first met him, I was the new kid in school, Later we became friends.

Me and Joe went riding our mini bikes everywhere, he had a Pow and I had a Gemini, one day we got the bright idea to take a handful of pain pills thinking that we can go riding and not get hurt, or not feel the pain, and we went out doing crazy stunts and we crashed and it hurt. One night at Gilbert's house I got the bright idea to through oranges at cars on the interstate. Joe joined me as we bombarded the cars, we were having a blast, we even went for another box of oranges, then this cargo truck was slowing, we thought we would really cream this truck then it stopped and shined a spot light on us, that's when we ran into the orange grove to get away. We were running as fast as we could in the darkness and I heard something behind us, we stopped and turned around, there was eyes shinning in the dark, it was a large herd of cows running after us, and they stopped at the same time as we did looking at us, so we turned and ran even harder knowing that we could be trampled at any moment, the sound of their steps were close behind us, we finally made it to the fence and jumped over it ripping our clothes and all the cows were right there, we barely made it out of their path. The next day we came back and everyone was mad at us, it turned out that the police came and wanted to arrest Gilbert because he had a headband on, I was wearing his headband that night, it was hard for the police to believe that it was not Gilbert, and the highway was dirty from all the oranges.

I thought highly of Joe he seemed so much smarter than me and he was so smooth with the girls. It was with Joe that I had most of my black outs so I can't remember much of the time that I spent with him except for the fact that I know we had fun. We used to go up to the earth tank and catch polliwogs. I was always impressed with how he could ride a wheelie for miles on his bicycle.

Joe and I went to Disneyland and went to Tom Sawyers island to smoke a joint we agreed that one would watch while the other smoked, I went in the bushes first then came a park ranger, he grabbed me and kicked me off the island, Joe did not warn me.

I was caught with pot many times but never got in trouble.

In order to get away for the whole weekend I would always tell my parents that I'm going camping with Joe so I wouldn't have to come back till Sunday night.

We used to get drunk and box each other but never in the face, we would just keep hitting each other until we were tired out. When Gerry my older brother would put on the gloves I would say no hitting in the face, and he would say OK, the first thing he would do is hit me in the nose, you'd think after two or three times I would learn my lesson but he kept on doing it so I never actually boxed my brother he just hit me in the nose.

The music that me and Joe would listen to was awesome, The Guess Who, and Paul McCartney RAM. We had lots of keg parties up at the monument overlooking El Capitan Mountain. Me and Joe spent most of our time at Gilberts house, that was always fun. I had a great time in my youth, good friends and good times, I will never forget them.

ALLAN

When I was riding with Alan on the back of my Honda 100 I was swerving back and forth down the road just playing around, Allen was hollering at me not to do it, so I straitened up, we were going about 50 mph when the front fender came loose and it slid around front tire making it like a ski, we hit the pavement, slid, rolled and bounced until we came to a stop, we were all busted up, sorry Alan. Onetime Allan had the idea to put a pulley on an electric pole cable and ride down the cable,

I joined in whole heartedly we climbed up hooked on and shot down the cable and landed in the branches of a tree to stop before hitting the next pole.

Allan and I decided to climb up El Capitan Mountain, we planned to climb up in one day and spend the night, and all our partying friends would be at the monument across the valley to see us. We packed our stuff and drove near to the base of the mountain, Allan brought his big dog Refer and I didn't think much about it until we were trying to climb strait up rock faces, we had to pull the dog up with a rope. By afternoon we were getting very tired of dragging this dog up the cliffs. Allan brought no water and I only had one little canteen, we both had strapped to our packs a gallon of wine in a glass bottle, while climbing Allan's bottle smashed against a rock. Well the night had finally come and we had not made it to the top, so we found a place to camp, we drank the wine and yelled out to our friends at the monument across the valley. That morning we were very dehydrated, all that I had was a can of chicken noodle soup so we shared it and decided not to continue up the mountain. Going down seemed to be harder than going up, and dehydration was hindering us. Just then a helicopter came and hovered over us, we waved our hands and hollered for help but the pilot just left and did not return. Then I decided to take drastic action, I found a gully washout next to us and jumped into it sliding down, running and tumbling desperately back down the mountain, at one point I stepped right over a diamond back rattle snake that was positioned to strike, I was moving so fast that it didn't have a chance, this became a scary race to get to water before it was too late. Well thank God we made it out alive. (Never bring a dog when climbing rock cliffs, and always bring enough water) Alan has turned out to be an awesome Christian man, I am at his house writing this book.

GILBERT

I spent most of my youth at Gilbert's house he was Jenny's older brother, he had a party room separate from his parent's house. Gilbert had a band called **The Electric Rainbow**; I really enjoyed their music, and just being with good friends. When we didn't have anything to do we would do things like make blow darts out of slick magazine pages and insert them into a half inch piece of p.v.c. pipe. Sometimes we put nails in the tips and shot them out the party room window at different targets,

we got pretty good. We were always getting as drunk and stoned as we possibly could, once on L.S.D. I was looking at the orange trees moving in the wind at night while the moon was shining upon them, I saw little monkey faces and they were all laughing at me, then I looked up at the stars and saw one that was throwing off sparks. When I looked at the carpet covering the wall the patterns started moving, and when someone would throw something you could see a trail behind it.

Once I was looking out the window and I saw a black horse and got the great idea to ride him, I came slowly up to him and was surprised that he didn't run away because he roamed free in a large orange grove, I jumped up on him and gave him a little kick, he started bucking uncontrollably, mabee because of no saddle or reins to control him, well he bucked until he lost control and fell backwards into an orange tree leaving me stuck in the branches all scratched up.

Once when I was really drunk and the room was spinning Gilbert started shooting me with his guitar which seemed to me at the time to be like a rifle killing me. After Gilbert lit his cigarette one time he threw the match at Jenny and her big bushy black hair went up in flames, he franticly put it out with his hands, and after she brushed her hair you couldn't even tell that it had been burnt. Many times we would be driving around in Gilbert's truck we were really drunk and he was driving on the wrong side of the road screaming obscenities out the window to wake people up in the middle of the night.

Gilbert sometimes would compete in motorcycle races, once he was at the starting line, looked down and noticed that he had a flat tire, the race started, so he went on and did the best he could, and he won the race, later I bought that motorcycle from him. Many times I would have to hide in the orange grove from Gilbert's mean old grandfather; I never could understand what he was saying or why he didn't want me around there.

One time I found Gil, lit a joint and smoked it with him; he said where did you get this; I said I picked your plant, dried it and rolled it, I don't think he liked that. Another time I handed him a joint that I had rolled up with pencil shavings when I was board at school, he lit it and coughed, he was so mad that he didn't give me a ride home from school that day.

For something to do we made hot air balloons, just a dry cleaning bag with birthday candles attached by straws, one time we sent two up at once and later on the radio news it was reported that U.F.O.s had been sighted.

BEFORE I WENT TO MEXICO

STOP RIDING IT

Some people have asked me in the past, how do you know that you hear from the Lord. I tell them some times he says yes, some times he says no and other times he says wait. For example; one night I was ridding my motorcycle home from work, enjoying the ride and thanking God for it. I don't hear his voice with my ears; he just puts it in my mind. While ridding along I heard **"Stop riding it"** I thought ok, if I have a near miss I'll know that I should stop riding it. **"No, stop ridding it"** I thought well that is just me saying that. Then I thought, no I would not say anything like that, so I knew it was the Lord. I sold the motorcycle and went four years without it, up to this point I had a motorbike all my life. After four years I came to a point where I could use a motorcycle again. I asked the Lord "can I have a motorcycle again?" He said **"Yes, you stopped riding just because I asked you to, you were faithful"** Thank you Jesus! I asked the Lord also; if this is true, could you help me find a used motorcycle, because all I have is $700.00 The next day a friend of a friend gave me a number of a bike for sale, I went, and he wanted $700. For a 750 Suzuki, I bought it on the spot, Thanks Lord. I really enjoy riding motorcycles.

THE OLD INTERNATIONAL

When my son Jeff and I would drive in my old international truck, many times the truck would not start, so Jeff and I would say a little prayer for the truck to start, and amazingly it would every time. One day I was loading logs that I cut and skinned for the cabin I was building, Jeff went to the bathroom back at the mobile home, by the time I finished loading the logs, he returned, ready to go and the truck did not start as usual, we said a little prayer, but this time it didn't start. I told Jeff, (he was 8 yrs old,) Some times the Lord says no because he knows something that we don't, So we went back to the trailer, upon entering I noticed two candles burning in the living room, he had lit them as his mother did for the smell, but he threw the whole wooden match stick into the candle and the heat from it broke the glass container so that the burning match flowed out with the wax onto the wood shelf. At this, I jumped for joy and hollered Praise the Lord! Jeff was scared, he thought he had done something wrong; I had to calm down to tell him about the miracle that just took place. The Lord kept us from leaving. If we had left, we would have returned to a puddle of aluminum and ashes. Thank You Jesus!

Once my son and I took a short cut in the wilderness and got lost, I couldn't even find where we entered, we were driving for it seemed like hours in my old international pickup and it was getting dark. I even used a crisscross pattern to find a way out. All the brake fluid leaked out, so I had to use gearing to slow down in this hilly area, we were running low on gas and it was getting dark, I was getting frantic, and jeff was getting scared, so we stopped and prayed, Lord please help us find a way out of here. Just a few minutes later we found a way out. Thank you Jesus! What an excellent friend to have!

HOW I MET THE LORD

I was raised as a devoted catholic, as I got older I believed that there was no God, and that Jesus was an alien dropped off here on earth to check out humans. One night in the Air Force, I was walking from the bar to the barracks, I walked into a light and felt the presence of the Lord all over me, I was amazed and overwhelmed by his power, more than drugs or alcohol , I knew who it was; it was Jesus! I was humbled in repentance. I don't even know how long I was there. I went back to the barracks and prayed for the first time in my life without a rosary, I did not know how to pray so I just asked the Lord Humbled in repentance; what do I do now? I couldn't sleep I was so excited. The next morning I heard a knock on the door, I opened the door and this dude stood there with a bible and asked me if I wanted to learn about the Lord, I was overwhelmed with joy and told him what happened the night before, he was amazed also, because he was used to people slamming the door in his face, which I would have done if not for the experience that I had the night before. His name was Mike Taylor, I studied with him once a week for a year. This is when I started a new life, when I cussed I felt bad about it, also with drugs, alcohol, cigarettes, cheating, lying, and stealing, I started making good changes in my life, smoking was the hardest to quit, but Jesus helped me. I started reading the bible, praying and going to church. Later as I was reading the bible I found that I needed to be baptized. Jesus said; "I say unto thee, except a man be born of water and of the Spirit, he cannot enter the kingdom of heaven." "He that believeth and is baptized shall be saved." "Baptism doth now save us." "Why tarriest thou? be baptized, and wash away thy sins, calling on the name of the Lord." "They were baptized in the name of the Lord Jesus."

After this experience I found out very quickly that there was someone did not like what happened to me, I found out later from reading the bible that it was Satan. He tried very hard to take away the joy and peace that the Lord had given me. Every time before I went to the weekly study with Mike I was down and depressed, that is how Satan wanted me to feel, but after being encouraged by Mike and the promises in the Bible I was filled with joy because I knew that Jesus loved me and forgave me of all my wrongdoings. Ye are of God little children and have overcome them because greater is he that is seeing you then he that is in the world.

BACKSLIDE

After a wonderful year of serving God and growing in the word, then Satan had his way with me; I went to a keg party down the hall in the barracks and got real sick. Now God had delivered me from these things that I had turned back to. Like a dog returns to his own vomit and sow having washed returns to her wallowing in the mire, but I knew the Lord still loved me. In my state of sin I still talked with the lord every day, I loved him but I didn't live a life that was pleasing to him thus I had no peace or joy in me. I lived in this state of depression for five years but I never forgot what the Lord had done for me.

MOTORCYCLE TRIPS

During this time I took my first vacation to California from the Air Force on my 500 dirt bike. I started a trip without a map and just headed west from Texas on an old cotton Road, this is the first time I ever drove on a long trip. After a couple days I stopped, bought a map and found out that I went way off course and down into El Paso but now that I had a map I found the interstate. I had my duffle bag strapped to the bike and I leaned back against it, I had my throttle locked in place so I could get real comfortable but when a big old truck passed me it almost blew me off the road. I finally made it to white sands New Mexico, it was terribly dry and hot, I made it to Arizona and it even got hotter, I stopped on the side of the road to sleep and used the curb for my pillow, after burning through the desert I made it to the Laguna Mountains where I froze crossing over, so when I finally arrived at my brother's house his wife answered the door and asked me who I was, she couldn't recognize me because I was burnt, frozen and tired. By the time I got there my tires were bald. On the way back I almost hit a cow in the road; my dirt bike headlight was very dim. If I would hit it at that speed I may not have survived.

Another time I was riding my 500 dirt bike in tall grass and I really couldn't see what was in front of me, I was going too fast as usual and flew off this 8 foot bank into a creek, the motorcycle did a nosedive and landed in the deep part of the creek but I landed on my head in the sand under the water, it felt like my neck was broken being shoved in like a turtle. I overcame the pain and swam under the water to get my motorcycle out, I finally dragged it out and it would not start, I was very far from the Air Force Base. I found someone with a car near by and tied a rope to the back of his car and drug my motorcycle down the road for a couple hours until it finally started.

I took a road trip to Colorado on my brand new 750 Honda with my wife Cindy on the back, I didn't have a windshield so the wind was blowing my helmet back and all the bugs were hitting my face, it was a long hard trip I don't ever want ride a motorcycle without a windshield again.

After that we went back with our dirt bikes and rode up to Pike's Peak with our motorcycle riding dog, at one point the clouds seemed to move violently around us. We went to the top and threw snowballs at each other in the middle of summer.

It was Halloween night on that same motorcycle in town that we stopped at a light and there was a cotton wagon hayride full of people drinking beer, while we were looking at them the person driving behind this was looking at them also and didn't see us, they ran right into us and knocked us off the motorcycle as the light turned green and the motorcycle was smashed underneath the hayride wagon. The credit union that I got the loan from for the bike required insurance that they had, so they bought me a new bike.

When I got out of the Air Force my brother-in-law Doug told me about some property in Arkansas on a creek. So I got my 500 dirt bike and headed out, it was 23° in Lubbock, Texas, and by the time I made it to Amarillo it was snowing about a foot on the sides of the roads. I tried to keep my hands warm by put them on the motor and after a while the threads from the gloves burned through and then cold air was going into my gloves. I finally made it to Arkansas found Doug and the land he was talking about and I fell in love with it, I didn't know you could still own a piece of property that had a creek, so I bought it and headed back. On the way back it wasn't as cold but it started to rain, I had no windshield and the rain drops were hitting me like rocks, I stopped at a rest stop and as I was leaving the bathroom I saw a guy get into his truck, I asked him if I could pay him to let me put my motorcycle in the back of his truck and bring me as far as he was going; he said OK, so we loaded up and he brought me as far as Oklahoma City and from there I rode the rest of the way. I try not to make long journeys on motorcycles anymore. After all these journeys the 500 stopped running well so I took the engine apart and found that the cam for the exost valve was worn down, I didn't have the money for a new one so I welded it and smoothed it off and put it back in, it worked great.

During these five years of wallowing in the Mire I would ask things of the Lord, like please give me a wife. He did! My wife Cindy had a religious back ground but she did not know the Lord Jesus, so we lived a worldly life together, strange thing though, I told Cindy before I married her that God would always come first, it is strange because at that time God was not the most important thing in my life.

THE ANGRY MAN

Once when we were living in a 4 x 12 foot trailer that I had built, parked near a railroad track in Maryland we were trying to earn enough money to rent an apartment. One day when Cindy was at work an old man came by walking his dog, I waved to him hello, he then proceeded to cuss me out for being a dirty lowdown hobo and that I was stinking up the neighborhood, he said he was going to call the police. As I was sitting there I said little prayer, I asked God to look down on this man and heal his heart and his hatred. The next day that old man came by and apologized, he brought a bible with one verse underlined about helping those in need, he kept coming back that day with blankets, firewood, warm clothes, money, and asked what else he could do for us. God changed his heart! This causes me to know that the Lord hears the prayers of everyone. I was not living a life that was pleasing to God but he heard my prayer and answered with a miracle for that man's life, because he wanted to, not because of anything I did.

Many times when I was at parties I would go lay down in the grass and talk to God looking into the sky, looking at the stars, thinking what a wondrous creation he has made for us to look upon. I remember one sunny day in Texas, I was riding the back of a pickup and I felt the love of Jesus all over me, I envisioned myself as a puppy at his feet full of joy wagging my tail. I remember one night in a bar, I was only half drunk, I felt him again and went outside to talk with him. I cried harder than I ever cried before not because of my sins but because he came down here and suffered and died for me, that is so sad, but I'm glad he did it so that I can be forgiven.

IN THE ARMY

One time this guy asked me about the Lord, I told him that the Lord is great, and he will change your life if you ask him to. I don't know if he understood me because he was my partying buddy and I was not living the example of a changed life, but I knew all this time that Jesus loved me. During this five years of being backslid and living in the world I did not learn much about the Lord but I was had great reverence for him, I prayed every day not so much asking forgiveness for my sinful ways but just thanking him for life health and everything else. At this time Satan had fooled me into thinking that getting drunk and doing drugs is okay with him. I would have the parties at the cabin thinking that they would give joy or purpose in life but they didn't. At this time I joined the Army, this was not enjoyable but the Lord knows everything. Thank God I didn't have to go to basic training again because I had rank from the Air Force. Because of my rank they made me squad leader of 37 men and I could barely remember how to march, I did my best marching them to tunes like Do Wa Ditty and other classics that I converted to a marching songs, a few times I marched them in right to a wall. But winter came and it was hard, we had to camp out in tents, in the woods, in the snow, for a couple of weeks. The worst part of this period was when I found myself in a slushy ditch, in the dark, in the water and ice and now I was ordered to clean my M-16, I was freezing and I could not see very good and with mud and slush on my frozen hands. Thank God I made it through that. Being a leader of 37 men is not an easy job but when the men would start complaining about something that I wanted them to do I just told them that I would quit and let my assistant platoon leader takeover, no one liked him, so they straightened out and did what I said, I always led them by example and helped them do everything. One day they took us to the field, we tied ropes around our wastes and climbed up a tall tower, when I got to the edge and looked down I was scared, that's when the drill sergeant pushed me off, after that I enjoyed repelling, I went back for more. I always enjoyed the confidence courses, it was like a playground for adults to me. I don't know how but I made honor graduate. After leaving training I was moved to an artillery base in Oklahoma, I found out that the regular army is a lot different than training, everyone had a bad attitude, I can see why. One time the commander had us walking in front of his Jeep checking for land mines with our feet in a chemical suit and mask in the blazing hot sun.

One time when our battalion went out to the field no one brought cigarettes so I found a bunch of old butts and took out the tobacco, everyone said how dumb that was, but after I rolled it up in a piece of newspaper and lit it, they all wanted some.

I learned some things in the Army that were beneficial but I was drinking heavily. I would keep a four dollar bottle of whiskey in the tool truck and drink it on duty, often. There was a threat of being tested for drugs so daily I had my son urinate in a cup, I put the urine in a surgical glove and hung around my waist. I would run almost two miles with this hanging on me in case they asked me to give a urine sample; it is amazing what someone will do in order to get high. After two years I was told that I was going to Germany, I did not want to go so I asked the first Sergeant if there was any way that I could get out of the army without getting a dishonorable discharge he said no, so I told him that I smoke pot. I was tested and sent to rehabilitation without disciplinary action. I wanted out now; I got caught drinking on duty on purpose in order to get out. This is when I really started seeking the Lord for help because when you get in trouble in the Army they really try to make your life miserable. The Lord heard my prayers and got me out faster than any of the others that were in trouble. Thank you Jesus!   I don't know why the Lord loved me through all that sin. I even got an honorable discharge.

REDEDICATED MY LIFE

When we moved back to Arkansas after building a cabin in Oklahoma, I wanted my son to go to Sunday school, so I was just going to drop him off their, but I found out that you don't just do that, so Cindy, Jeff and I went to church. I don't know how Cindy felt, but as soon as the preaching started I was overwhelmed at the presence of God, I had never heard anything like this. I had never known the Pentecostal way, I ran to the alter before the preacher was even finished and gave my life back to Jesus wholeheartedly, the Lord turned me from my sinful ways that day. Praise God Cindy gave her heart to the Lord two weeks later. Now this part is very important; I had salvation by the promise of God's Word through the remission of sin and I was living a life that was pleasing to God. I found out through the word that there was more to receive from God if I wanted, the promise Jesus gave before he went up to heaven. The comforter which is the Holy Ghost, and ye shall receive power when the Holy Ghost is come upon you and he shall be witnesses unto me. I went to the altar seeking after this Holy Ghost that I had read about, I did not receive it then, but I kept trying and praying at home for this power that would help me live a righteous life, pleasing to God. Then after three weeks I was at the altar praising God, and suddenly strange words started coming out of my mouth, immediately I thought, this is not of God, but I realized that Satan did not want me to have this power, he tried to convince me that this was not real, so then I knew that it was real because Satan tried to interfere with me receiving it. I have found that what ever is pleasing to God, Satan does not want you to do it. Now with this extra power I was armed and ready for effective service to God in the name of Jesus Christ. I went out right away and knocked on every door in the community to tell them about Jesus and what he done for me. Now that I had this Holy Ghost power I realized how unhappy I was before when I was living in the world trying to fill the void in my life with drugs, alcohol, and parties. I have real joy now, I am the happiest man I know. One morning we went to church and came home to find our house on fire, I tried to put it out with a gravity flow garden hose but there was not enough pressure, when I open the front door it almost sucked me in, so I closed the door, sat down and watched it burn. Sitting there I read some scriptures that comforted me. The Lord is good, a stronghold in the day of trouble, he knows then trust in him. After the cabin burned we lived in a borrowed bus behind a friend's house. Since then I have rebuilt the cabin and it is twice as big and twice as good as the way it was, I even built a castle on the front of it.

SPRINKLER SYSTEM JOB

After this, I got a job and had to travel out-of-state weeks at a time, I wanted to tell people about Jesus but was afraid, I would go up to someone on the job and want to tell them that Jesus loved them but I couldn't, this was frustrating making me. I prayed earnestly about it and the Lord gave me this scripture. For the Lord has not given us a spirit of fear but of power and love and a sound mind. The next morning we were eating breakfast at a restaurant before going to work, next to me I heard this lady going on about how miserable she was, and I was full of joy from the Lord. So I stood up and said to all the people; can I have your attention please, Jesus loves you and wants to change your life, and he will, if you let him. My boss did not like that at all. From that time on till now I have not been afraid to ever say anything to anyone about Jesus.

One time I was at work doing a very tedious job, putting pipe dope on sprinkler heads, I was praying and praising God in such a spiritual way that I left my body and hovered about 15 feet above myself. This may be hard for anyone to believe in but it was then that I realized that this body is just a temporary place that we live and this life need not be controlled by the desires of our flesh but by the guidance of the spirit.

When I was working down in Lake Charles Louisiana I applied for a job at Bowing Aircraft that was being built there. They accepted my application and I was to start school in three weeks as an aircraft quality control inspector, it was a real good pay and a nice place to live. I came home and told Cindy about it, she said that she would not go. I was determined to take this good opportunity, I set my mind to go, I prayed and ask God for his will, I told him that I needed an answer by today. If no answer I would go, but a while later that day God just changed my mind, I thought; why would I want to leave here. Isn't it great that when his will is against ours he will make us happy with his will? If I went there is no telling how miserable I would have been. (I had no job at the time)

CABIN BURNED DOWN

In those days after our home burned with no insurance living in a bus behind a friend's house, having jobs with low pay, we were blessed by God in that we'd bought two acres of land and put a mobile home on it, we went from having nothing to having a blessed life in a matter of months! Thank you Jesus. It was then that I wondered if I would still serve God and if I would still feel as close to him if I was to receive abundant material blessings. I felt then that it was a lot easier to be close to God without all the things in this world to interfere with my relationship with him. It seems that our possessions take all of our time and all of our concerns are on them.

PALLET YARD JOB

I got a job at the pallet yard; it was there that I had trouble with people who hated church and the Bible. They would rip the day the scriptures down that I put on a bulletin board, throw them down on the floor and stomp on them. I was told that if I continued to talk about the Lord that they would have to let me go. I kept on and they did not fire me!

I started fasting for the first time in my life, this brought spiritual power and authority over the flesh. I would go to the Park and worship God at lunch. One morning at work a guy asked me if I wanted to smoke a joint with him, I said; that would ruin my buzz because I'm high on the Lord. I don't think he understood, how could he, he did not know God who gives joy unspeakable and full of glory. (Later on this guy ended up getting killed, drunk driving)

Going to church was great, more fun than any party that I ever went to, we would stay for hours, worship God and edify each other in the Lord. I would leave church so happy and full of joy that I would go around in the neighborhood and tell people of the great and wonderful things God is doing in the church. Once I went to an old friend's house that I used to party with, just to visit. I was living for the Lord and had no need of worldly pleasures but for some reason when he offered me some of his joint I took some. Suddenly I felt conviction all over me and a mighty reverence for God, I immediately went outside to worship him and talk with him for hours till way past dark, I felt so close to God talking with him like Abraham did. What a wondrous joy revealing to me many mysteries. That night I built an altar in the dark it must have weighed 800 pounds. I went back to my friend's house; they asked what had happened to me? They could see it on my face, I had been talking to God, and they were bewildered by this, they knowing about God but not really knowing him.

CABIN REBUILD

After work each day we started rebuilding the cabin, when I say we I mean me and Jesus. When I would talk to myself I would say things like we and us, I still do. If not for the Lord's help I could not have done the things that I did, things that one man alone could not do. One time the rope broke and I fell off the two-story roof, I landed on my backside on a sharp rock, this would have been very painful if it wasn't for that Bible in my pocket to cushion the impact.

Once I When I was working on the log walls of the cabin I had to cut off the ends evenly, I was standing about the twenty feet above a very rocky terrain on a cliff,

suddenly the bottom log that I was standing on broke, the 20 inch insert chainsaw went flying, I landed on my back out of breath, praying; take the pain Jesus, he did! Only by his grace did I live and not have permanent injuries. Many times I lifted more than his body is able, thank you Jesus for being with me in times of hardship and in times of joy, you are my best friend!

HEALING

Over the many years I have trusted the Lord for healing, he has healed me of things that the doctors and medicine could not fix, because of this I have great faith that he has given me to believe in continued healing. He healed me of ear and throat infections, bursitis, arthritis, tendonitis and all other pains that plagued me but most of all he healed me of devilitis.

One night I was at work and started feeling very sick, I didn't know when to sit on the pot or bend over it, aching muscles, sensitive skin, and all the symptoms of the flu. 12 p.m. it was time to go home, as I left the heated shop I was too cold, it was 34°F outside. I got on a motorcycle and off I went, I was so cold I was hurting down to the marrow of my bones, I had 35 miles to go at 65 mph, after a couple of miles I started praying to the Lord that he would have mercy on me, soon I started speaking in another tongue as the Spirit gave me utterance, my prayers became louder and louder then the prayer changed from having mercy on me, to shouts of praise and joy. Then warmth filled my body and soul, I don't know how many people I woke up by shouting praises unto God in the middle of the night but I could not help it. When I got home I was warmer than I was while I was sitting in the shop. I thanked my God and my best friend for his goodness to me. Then I thought to myself that the Lord got me home in comfort but tomorrow I will probably be deathly sick because of being in the cold. The next day I felt incredible, awesome and totally healed.

TRIALS

One morning I got up and found that I had a leaking pipe in my home, so the floor and carpet were soaked; I tore up the carpet and fixed the water leak. Now I was ready to go to work, my car would not start, I put the battery on the charger and said; I will just ride the motorcycle, the tire was flat, during this time I was not getting angry like sometimes when things go wrong for me, I just went on from one thing to the next with a song in my heart that the Lord gave me. Well I got a flat tire fixed and started off to work; halfway there I ran out of gas, I pushed the motorcycle one mile to the gas station. I went to return the three movies that I had rented to the Christian bookstore, when I got there I found that the tapes were gone. I started backtracking about 15 miles looking for the tapes but could not find them, I went back to the store and told them that I lost the tapes, I had to pay $60 and then I headed off to work noticing that my chain was popping and about to come off the sprocket. I made to work on time, thanks Lord! The store called later and said that someone had found the tapes, they were a little muddy but I could come and get my refund. It is amazing that I have peace and joy in times of trouble and great rewards after going through them, how can people say that they can't live for the Lord when he makes life so much easier?

POWER OF GOD

A friend of mine made a decision to serve the Lord at church around Christmas time. I had been noticing that many people forgot what God did at the altar and their lives remain the same with no change, so I started praying and fasting that this would not happen to him. I only planned to fast for two days but the Lord led me to fast longer. On New Year's Eve after we had lit the fireworks, all four of us decided to gather around and pray for each other and the New Year. We all started feeling the presence of God; each one of us went to pray in the yard under the stars. We all felt the presence of the Lord grow more powerful, then I felt led to lay hands on my friend, when I'd did; he started speaking very loudly in another language that sounded Arabic, this overwhelmed me with the glory of God like I had never felt before, so great it was that we could not stand or even kneel before the great almighty glory and power of God. God's power felt so great over me that I felt like a worm under his foot. I was completely amazed that Andy could bear to receive this much glory. After an hour of being blessed with his powerful presence I felt that my body could not take it anymore, so I asked God to mellow me out, but he was not finished. For another hour we were completely immersed in the great powerful presence of the Holy Ghost, rolling in the dirt praising him. I felt as close to God is Abraham and Moses, men who walked with God, I felt like I could fly, at the same time I felt that my body would completely give out because of the overwhelming power of his glory. Our language cannot describe his glory. Between us we were used in four different gifts of the Holy Ghost as described in the Bible   1.Different kinds of tongues 2. Message in tongues 3. Interpretation of tongues 4. The gift of prophecy. In two of these gifts we had never been used before. When the Lord finally released us from the power of his glory we went to lay hands on everyone we could find but it was two thirty in the morning. It took hours for us to finally mellow out and go to sleep.

The next day we went to church and that evening we found people who we had invited showed up and wanted prayer at the end of the service. There was two messages in tongues given and two interpretations, then a third message but no interpretation, then Andy who had just received the Holy Ghost, and knew nothing about the gifts or how they operated in the church, gave a repeat for the message not knowing that he was being used in another gift of the Holy Ghost, then it was interpreted. Also the Holy Ghost took control of the whole event. Andy not knowing how the Holy Ghost operated with order, hushed when the messages were given. God is amazing. Also later when we were waiting in the car to go home we felt that we should go back in the church, they were still praying so we joined them. Then I was led to get one more person who was still waiting in the car to see if she wanted to come in and meet the Lord. She did. It turned out that the Holy Ghost would not let us leave before all these things had taken place. There were many things that were accomplished that were not seen, but we knew that our requests were being granted through faith and confirmation of the Holy Ghost. Thus the whole weekend was amazing, powerful and filled with glory and we were awestruck by God's presence through the power of the Holy Ghost. We were strengthened over our sinful minds, also we were given a work to do, which we'd boldly went out to do without doubt, fear, reluctance or laziness giving our all to God and his purpose holding back nothing. For what more is there to this life than to please the one who gave us life. Glory to God forever and ever!

CHEST HAIRS

I know as a Christian that should turn the other cheek, but I was having trouble with my lead man at work, he kept pulling my chest hairs, this was very painful to me. I told him in a very serious tone of voice; do not do that again. The next night at work he came by and did it again, now this had been going on for some time now and it wasn't so much that I was angry or wanted to strike back, I just wanted him to stop. He knew that he could do these things to me because he knew that I was a Christian and should allow it to go on. One night when he did it again, he was standing very close to me and everyone around was watching to see what a Christian would do. I firmly planted my elbow into his chest without anyone seeing, as he bent over in pain I put my hand on his shoulder and asked him if he was all right, as if I did not know what was wrong with him, and he was too embarrassed to tell anyone what I had done, he never messed with this Christian again! Thank you Lord for helping me out of that situation without discrediting you.

One night when I got off work and rode my motorcycle home, I felt God's presence in me and all around me. My prayers to him or anointed, speaking the wondrous mysteries of the Gospel. I got home and was going to pray and go to bed like I usually did but I could not stop praying at the side of my bed, so I decided to go outside and pray under the starry sky, what a peace and what joy was all over me. I decided after about an hour to spend the night outside with God. I got my blankets and spent the night on the top of the Winnebago talking with God like a friend with great peace and joy.

ROYAL RANGERS

At this time the Lord blessed me with service in the royal Rangers, teaching young people. The Lord gave me the desire to lead them away from drugs, alcohol, sex and worldly things, and to the peace and joy of being a child of God. I did not have an opportunity to know the Lord when I was young. The Lord blessed me with many ideas and material to teach in an effective way.

One time at a district royal ranger camp out, the campfire altar call had been given but none of the kids were responding, the Lord poked me telling me to go forward and say something but I said no, the Lord poked me again, I had to go now, so I step down to the front, it was very quiet, the pastor had been waiting for some time. I asked the preacher if it was all right to speak with them, he seemed very glad that I asked and said go-ahead, I started speaking to them under the anointing of the Holy Ghost, I don't know what I said but praise God all the kids young and old came forward to receive Jesus and some to rededicate their lives. That was the first time the Lord ever anointed me to speak with boldness, it felt so good that I could not contain myself for joy; I jumped for joy and ran like a wild animal in the desert when the rain comes after the drought.

In order to keep the royal ranger meetings interesting for the kids the Lord helped me think of things for us to do like repelling, exploring caves, hiking, camping, canoeing and swimming, I even built a military confidence course for them to challenge themselves. We had fire competitions; who could burn the string first, we shot pistols, rifles and archery.

One time we were camping in the mountains 90 miles away from home, I lost my car keys while swimming in water about fifteen feet deep, there were six teenagers with me, we all looked very hard for the keys, we searched for a long time and it was getting dark, so we all gathered together and prayed, five minutes later I found keys at the bottom of the swimming hole. God is good!

I was watching some videos of skateboarders doing their tricks on a half pipe, so I decided to build one for me and the kids. After it was built I new from watching the videos that I could do this, so I got up on flat part of the platform and rolled my skateboard off, I fell like a ton of bricks, I was hurting from more than a week from that, it is not as easy as it looks on the videos.

After a short time more kids came, so many, that we had to split the meetings, young kids on Saturday and the older ones on Sunday. All the kids had to pass a test on the Bible every week in order to keep coming to the meetings. There was no support from the church that I was going to, I had to pay my own insurance also. I was told that every parent had to sign papers saying that the church could not be held responsible for the youth activities. Some from the church even went about advising that parents not let their kids go to the meetings. All these things did not hinder the Lord's work, more kids were coming to the meetings and many parents were getting interested in the program. This may seem like a time of trials for me, but I loved it, I drew closer to the Lord when I was serving him with opposition. I worked real hard and tried to be a good example hoping that the church would accept me in the work that the Lord called me to do, I studied hard passed courses in guiding youth and grew strong in the Lord as a new Christian and good relations with the people of the community. Upon my return from national royal ranger training camp in Missouri I was full of joy and plans for the royal ranger meetings. Then to my surprise I was dismissed from the program by the pastor who was backslid and part of the church board. There was approximately 30 kids coming to the meetings at the time and I was bringing them to Sunday school. I decided after seeking the Lord in prayer to continue the program under another name; "kids for Christ". By the grace of God

I held these meetings for a total of five years with only one accident, one kid got mud in his eye. Now that could only be done if the Lord was in it! Thank you Lord, I have no resentment towards anyone at all, because the Lord Jesus has filled my heart with love and the Holy Ghost.

TYSON JOB

After that the Lord blessed me with a better job than building pallets, I got a job in a freezer operating a forklift where I was able to share the joy of the Lord with many people, I put scriptures on the bulletin board and no one tore them down. I was always reading my Bible at break time so this one backslid preacher I knew named me; "The Bible man". Then there was a job in the maintenance department, 38 people signed up for the job, two guys were sure that they would get it. I wanted to be in the maintenance department so I asked the Lord that his will be done and what ever it is I will be content. They picked me, my supervisor asked how I got the job, and I said the Lord gave it to me!

I later transferred to the Clarksville plant and one morning of my first week I was told to go check out the sump pumps, I put my tall boots on and went out to find that the whole area was flooded, I went inside the pump room and saw my supervisor there, he said nothing as I walked toward him in six inches of blood. I took one more step and fell into the blood pit up to my chin in blood, the grating was removed, I could have been ripped open from the edge of the grating around the pit. My supervisor just laughed as I pulled myself out, then he ran off not speaking a word to me, he went to tell everyone in the shop so they could laugh about it also. I went home to wash off but could not get the blood smell of me for a weak and I had to through my uniform away.

DREAMS

I have had two real neat dreams about the Lord, four years apart. In the first one I was lying on a friends front lawn looking at the stars above praising God as I often did for real but in this dream as I was lying there, suddenly the stars shot out of sight, two or three at a time until the sky was starless, then a shadow in the form of a ceiling tile lowered down to about 100 feet above me, then I started floating up. I thought this must be the catching up, filled with joy I started rising up through the frame but when I got about halfway through I felt a great desire to return and tell everyone about God. I went back down and was running through the streets saying; it's the rapture! Praise God! When I even spoke of the name of Jesus people fell down and repented. Everyone was running around excited about the Lord and there was such joy! Then I woke up.

The second dream I had, I was sitting with my wife and son and around church that was full of people, everyone that wanted healing was to stand against the outer walls facing it, and I felt that my back needed healing so I went, as I waited to be prayed for it felt like someone punched me real hard in the lower back, it felt like his fist went into my back, I was shocked at first thinking that it would hurt, then warmth spread from that point and filled my body, then knew that I was healed! And I woke up.

In another, I was on a military mission in the deserts of Iraq and a sand storm overtook us, I was lost from my fellow soldiers, I tried to follow the tire tracts in the sand but they had disappeared, after a while I saw some enemy soldiers and tried to hide but they found me and brought me to an Al Qaeda training camp where they kept me in a small tin shack then they came and cut my toes off with an ax. Every day they would come to beat me and just make life miserable but I found myself loving them like Jesus loves me. After my feet had healed they would come to box with me because I had told them how I enjoyed boxing, after a while they saw in me something that their religion did not offer them, it was love, forgiveness and a personal relationship with their God. Then I woke up.

MY WIFE CINDY

One day when I was working on a jet engine afterburner I looked up and saw this beautiful girl, she was the new parts girl. I knew from that moment I wanted to make her mine, I was still very shy not learning the lessons from my first girlfriend so I didn't know how to speak to her. So I moved into a tent next door to the trailer that she was living in with two of her male friends, I got to know them which made it easier to know her. We started jogging to work every day, and we got to know each other, she was very outgoing like me. We went to an April Wine concert and that's where I told her that I loved her, but she didn't hear me because the music was too loud, I took it as total rejection, then she wanted to know what was wrong with me and invited me to go down closer to the stage, standing there feeling rejected Cindy slipped her hand into mine, that felt so wonderful. We started spending a lot more time together. She was tired of the Air Force guys that she was sharing a trailer with, so I suggested that we get an apartment together, so we did, and I asked her to marry me, she said yes. We did lots of fun things like hiking, swimming, camping, and lots of partying. We bought a house in the city that cost way too much, after about a year I decided to build a self-sufficient trailer in the front yard, so when our son was born we moved into it and moved it to a cotton field close to the Air Force Base, my father-in-law was not impressed. The water heater was wood burning and the water pressure was pumped up by a bicycle air pump. The electricity was only 12 volts and we had to haul water in, but Cindy gladly moved out there with me, in fact I think it was the closest time we had together in our marriage. After getting out of the Air Force I bought a piece of land in Arkansas next to a creek and started building a rock cabin. After living in the cabin for awhile I felt like we need a bigger piece of land, so I joined the Army to get enough money to buy a bigger piece of land, this was a mistake. I was always drunk in the Army. After I got out we bought twenty acres of land near Sallisaw Oklahoma in the woods with no electricity, bad roads and we had to haul water in. We started building another rock cabin. Cindy gladly went with me; she really must have loved me to go through all that. After the hard work of building a rock cabin we moved back to Arkansas and started going to church, that is when the cabin burned down. While we were living in a bus because of no place else to live Cindy said; "I don't think I love you anymore". That went in one year and out the other, I couldn't believe she even said it, I guess that's why I didn't pay attention, I didn't listen, I didn't ask her why. That is the point where I lost her love and I didn't know it, I should have known, I could have tried to figure out what was wrong but I just went on like nothing had happened. That was a big mistake that I hope never to make again. We were together six more years and she did not love me, there was nothing I could do to make her love me, I tried and tried but it did not work. So eventually we got a divorce. I still loved her for eight years after the divorce until I met Reina in Mexico.

When Cindy moved away my son Jeff went with her, they moved to Texas near Houston first, I moved all their stuff down there in the crummy old van and a trailer that was in worse shape. I looked for a job while I was there so I could be around my son, but there were no jobs. After I returned to my job in Arkansas I had an ulcer, and I couldn't figure out why, I wasn't under any stress, but my coworkers said didn't you just come back from a hard stressful trip? Yes, I thought, I did. It is amazing how the mind can work completely separate from the body. After this they moved back to Arkansas, thank God I could be with my son again, teaching him about the Lord and going to church. After that they moved to Maryland which was very far away, I looked for a job there also in order to be with my son, no jobs. It is there that my son started using drugs and alcohol, smoking cigarettes, and he crashed his car's various times. One-time when I came to visit it seemed that he had no respect for his dad, I don't think he even want to spend any time with me. Later he ended up in a halfway house and that's where the police came to arrest him for armed robbery, and he ended up in jail. After a while in jail he came back to the Lord and wrote me a fantastic letter, saying; how I had been an example for him. I was jumping up and down with joy in the post office and then I read before the whole church, we all had been praying for him. I went to visit him just after he got out of jail and it was like I had my son back again, it was wonderful just hanging around with him. Now he is going to Bible College, he wants to be a youth pastor, he is so smart and learning so much, I am very proud of him. Thank you Jesus for hearing my prayers and turning bad into good.

MY SON JEFF

The best times of my Christian life were spent with Jeff; we did everything together, things that I would not normally do. When I was with him I felt young again and wanted to do all those thrill seeking things that kids do. We went to a lake east of Russellville Ar. and took a little boat over to the overflow tower and jumped off of it into the water, after a while we went to see where the water was coming out at the bottom of the dam, it was about a four foot pipe, we went in but it was too dark so we went and got some flashlights. When we returned with some of Jeff's friends we were ready to explore, this tunnel was deep, over a football field long, we were walking in water about six inches deep. After exploring to the end where the water fell in I got an idea to go about midway through the tunnel and block the water off with our bodies, about five of us laid down together and backed up the water behind us until we could not hold it back any longer.

I remember laughing so hard that I could barely breathe, then I said; break loose, and we all floated through the pipe like flushing the toilet and shot out the end of it falling about five feet into the overflow pond, we did this over and over until we were exosted.

We went riding our bicycles around in the city of Little Rock as we had done in other cities just exploring, we took our bikes onto the parking lot elevators and rode our bikes down as fast as we could, on skateboards also. While ridding around we ended up by the Arkansas river and we heard water falling near the edge, we went to investigate, it was a huge drainage pipe ten feet in diameter with about five inches of water flowing out of it, we had to explore this, so we went for flashlights and rope. Arriving with supplies and one of Jeff's friends we lowered the bikes down to the tunnel with the rope then I climbed up the fixed steel ladder to the entrance, threw down the rope and pulled the bikes up inside. I only had two flashlights so I held them both, one shining back for Nathan and one forward for Jeff, but when I started riding up and down the sides of the concrete tunnel they would loose light for a moment. About a mile in and we heard water falling it must have been running off of a street because it was hot, we played in that for a while. As we went on the tunnel got smaller and smaller, it also branched off many times, we would look into the side tunnels, and in one tunnel we saw light so we went in, at the end of it we stuck our heads out and found that we were in the middle of the interstate looking back at Little Rock from the other side about eight miles from where we entered. As we reached the end of the tunnels I came out into a park and there was two old guys there drinking some wine and they asked me; where did you come from; and I said; from visiting the teenage mutant ninja turtles, they did not believe it until they saw me return to the drainage hole and enter. Later that evening we went riding at McCain Mall and we found these tarps that covered the plaza, they were about fifty feet tall at the top point, so when it got dark and everyone left, we climbed up on them and jumped like on a trampoline, it was scary but fun, then we slid down them but we had to use some clothes to hold on to the cable without burning our hands because if you went too fast you would not be able to stop before falling off the edge, we did this for hours. Later that night as we were riding around we found some kids that had the idea of going swimming at the city public pool at 2 A.M. in the morning, so we went with them. We climbed the fence and got in, and we had a blast for about an hour, jumping off the high dive in the dark, I could only see the water as the light glittered off of it. We finally went home, it was a long day.

While riding around in Russellville we stopped at the hospital and went in to explore, it was under construction and we could not go up to the fourth floor in order to look off the roof. I found a garden hose in the yard on the side of the building and tied it around Jeff, I took the other end and climbed up the rain gutter to the roof, I pulled Jeff up with the hose. After we were up there walking around the construction men wondered how and why we were there, I just acted like a construction boss that was showing my son around the job site and no one gave me trouble. We left through the door that we could not enter from the outside.

Another sunny day in the same town we went ridding through the open concrete drainage ditches, a few hours later it started to rain very heavily but we kept ridding in the water as it began to rise then it became a fun challenge to see just how deep of water we could ride in. When the water rose up to our chests, Jeff lost his bike in the strong current, I swam down to feel for the bike but couldn't find it, now Jeff was suffering hypothermia so I brought him to a near by laundry matt while I continued

looking for his new bike, I searched way down stream thinking that the current had taken it but after a couple hours I found it right where he lost it now that the water had risen to five feet.

As we went Rock climbing and repelling we were always looking for something harder and higher, On sky line drive overlooking the river we found a cliff about eighty-five feet high, the thing that was special about this cliff was that about half way down there was a pillar of rock just out from the cliff, we could get a running start and jump off of it swinging around to the other side of the cliff.

Another cliff we found was about a hundred and twenty feet high, I was scared to step off the ledge but once I was on the side I could run back and forth on the wall about thirty feet. Once we were at the bottom we found a ledge that went up under the cliff, so we climbed up inside still hooked to the rope and jumped swinging out over the creek. When one of my friend tried it he jumped but the rope hooked on a rock about ten feet above him which cut his swing short, hurling him upward then the rock broke off and he fell bouncing to almost hit the ground.

Then we got the idea to repel off bridges, which is where Jeff did his finest repelling. After a while I tried tying off to the middle of the bridge then carefully moving out the edge to about thirty feet from where I tied off then jump, I could hardly stay sitting up in the harness from the G-Force in the middle of the swing,

then from the momentum I slammed up under the bottom of the bridge and this was at night.

One time we had climbed up on an old water tank, we were looking around with the binoculars and saw a really tall water tank overlooking Clarksville so we set out to find it, that took a couple of hours, when we got there we found that it was a new tank and they had not put a fence around it yet so we started climbing, Jeff went first so that if he fell I could catch him, about half way up I was getting scared, about three quarters the way there was a valve, I opened it and water came out that really scared me, I wanted to go back down but Jeff kept going up so I stayed with him and we made it to the top, we were so high up that cars on the interstate looked like ants. The top was only about eight feet around, there was a door so I opened it and saw the water below, which made me dizzy with fear. The reason that we climbed up there was to repel down it, I had the idea of running around the tank while dangling on the rope but when I went off the edge I was too scared to run around it, I just went strait down to the ground. Jeff didn't repel down, he untied the rope and came down the ladder, I promise to never do that again!

A time before that we climbed an old fire tower in the mountains, it would sway in the wind but it wasn't enough to go up in the box, I had to climb up onto the roof of it. We repelled off of it also.

I wanted to dam up the creek at the cabin but there was a big rock that I couldn't move or break with a sledge hammer so I bought some dynamite. I took three sticks and wrapped it tight in tape, I shoved it under the rock and packed it in with rocks, I ran the hundred foot wire up the cliff to the truck battery, I touched the wires and boom! After that it was quiet so we started heading down to look when we heard tink, tink, I looked up and saw a huge rock coming down, I yelled out; HIDE! And dove under the truck, Jeff and Nathan ran into the shed just behind them. The rocks came crashing down on the truck and the shed, the windshield was smashed, after the rocks stopped falling we went down to see and the rock was completely gone. I heard some time later that my neighbor had rocks falling on his roof a quarter mile away. Well I built the dam and it made a real nice swimming hole but six years later

the core of engineers said that I could not dam up their creek. I told him that I left some cement out and those pesky beavers built the dam. He did not believe me. Later they tore it down.

We went to Little Piney Creek with a friend named Bill, we were dropped off by Cindy that hot morning at the upper bridge with my flat bottom aluminum boat, we were going to float the river down to the lower bridge and we expected to arrive that afternoon where Cindy would be waiting. As we started down the slow flowing creek we were enjoying all the natural sights, like the cliff edges and the dense forest, then we came to a shallow part in the creek, we had to get out of the boat and push it over the rocks until we got to the deeper part. As we went further there was less and less water, many times we had to lift the boat and carry it over the rocky parts, walking in the ankle high water we noticed that there were poisonous Cottonmouth snakes all around us and it was getting dark, we had no flashlights, we only planned for and afternoon trip but now it was too dark to continue, we tried to continue in the dark but just thinking about the snakes made it out of the question, so we stopped at a clearing to spend the night. I was so glad that Bill smoked, he had a lighter so we could light a fire, we had no blankets or pillows. I took the life vest and tore it in three pieces to use for pillows that made sleeping in the dirt a little more comfortable. Jeff and Bill fell right to sleep but I could not sleep, then I heard some branches breaking in the darkness of the forest, I just knew that it was a hungry bear, so then I did not sleep, also I was thinking about how worried Cindy was because we did not arrive. Finally the light of morning came and we started down the creek, we finally made it to the lower bridge that afternoon and Cindy was waiting.

Another time with the same boat we went up the rapids with a five horse motor, it was crazy, the water was cold and it kept splashing on Jeff while he was trying to hold the video camera, some parts of the rapids were so strong that going full throttle was not moving us forward very fast so we moved to the side. On that same creek we built a cable ride from a big tree into the water it was so high that I was scared to take the first ride but after I did everyone wanted to go down it.

We took a trip down the Big Piney in my old canoe, this time we brought supplies and planned to spend the night. We drove to where we were going to end the trip and left the motorcycle there, then we went about twenty miles north to start the trip. There was plenty of water here even some white water rapids, we stopped a lot to explore, climb up cliffs, and jump off rocks into the rapidly flowing water. After a day of floating we found a nice sandbar and stopped for the night, lit a fire and roasted hot dogs. It was so nice laying in the sand looking at the stars and being with my son. The next day we arrived at the motorcycle and went to get the truck. Some times we did do things without problems. We went canoeing and camping many times. One time while canoeing my kayak broke in half in the rapids.

Many times we went exploring on three-wheelers, one time ridding on the edge Arkansas River we came to a spot that a creek met the river, we thought our trail had come to an end, but we got the idea to see if the three-wheelers would float, they did so we swam pushing them along until we reached the other side, we always enjoyed a challenge to overcome.

On another three-wheeler trip we were racing through the woods when I heard a strange sound; bloop, bloop, plop, we stopped to investigate in the thick woods, we found a ten feet deep hole with mud and something was bubbling up through it, I went close to smell if it was gas but there was no smell. I really wanted to know what it was so we went to get some matches and returned, I lit a match and threw it in, nothing happened, I thought that mabee it went out so I lit a piece of paper and threw it in. Flames burst out of the hole about twenty feet high. We immediately went and called the gas company and told them about the fire and we waited for them, to show them where it was, when we got there he grabbed his little fire extinguisher and spayed it at the flame which blew it into a tree and it caught on fire, he obviously was not trained to put out fires, I told him I was, but he would not give me the extinguisher, he was frantic now and wanted me to go with him and leave my son there, I said; no way. So he left and so did we. He wondered how the gas was lit but I gave him no info about that.

Many times we would go to the woods and have paint ball wars, I would be against Jeff and Nathan, they would hunt me down or I would hunt them down. Our favorite place was on chimney rock road; there were cliffs, caverns and lots of places to hide. One time I was on the south cliff and I saw a forehead stick up just about an inch on the north cliff and I shot, Right between the eyes. We shot 22 pistols at targets also.

We went caving a lot also, in the bat cave we had to repel down in the dark and found some little holes that opened up into great caverns, we found this one room we called the clay room, people over the years had made many interesting sculptures we did too. The bat cave was muddy but copperhead cave was clean and had a creek flowing through it, we explored it all the way to the end, in one part of the cave there was a water slide. We were always looking for new caves.

HAWAI I

We took a vacation to Hawaii and spent ten thousand dollars in two weeks, we spared no expense. We cruised all over on scooters even up to the waterfall in the rain forest, we hopped islands on small planes, we went to the big island and rented a four wheel drive and hiked to see the volcano, we flew to another and snorkeled in the quarrel reef caves seeing who could swim the farthest before finding a hole to come out of, I got stuck in one hole under the water but managed to force my way through, we also bought fish food and the fish knew that we had it, they would attack us for it, there were many beautiful fish. Just across the road was a fresh water cave.

We went in with flashlights and found a cavern under the water. We stayed at real nice hotels, and went around picking fruit, Jeff had to have every fruit and pick it his own self.

One winter I took Jeff and the youth group out sliding around on the iced up roads, we ended up on the interstate four lanes to spin around on. I told the kids that if we lost control that you should get down on the floor of the van. Well I was loosing control on purpose and one kid named John stayed on the floor scarred out of his wits, we all survived and it was fun.

We would tie a rope to the back of the truck and pull people around on some old skis I had, we would ski off to the side and try not to hit a sign or land in a ditch.

When I went to visit Jeff and his mom in Maryland he took me snowboarding,
I borrowed his friend's board. When we got to the slope Jeff said; Dad don't be
discouraged if you don't learn in one day, it took me a few days to learn. We went
up and down the slopes all day and I fell a lot but at the end of the day we were at
the bottom of the slope, a man came up to me and said; I've been watching you and
your son, would you like a job teaching kids how to snowboard? I felt pretty good him
saying that right in front of Jeff, but after that I needed a vacation from my vacation
with him because I was hurting.

We took a helicopter ride and the pilot swooped down turning to the side and we
were pressed up against the glass looking strait down.

We flew in a small airplane and Jeff wanted to fly through a cloud so the pilot took
us through, it was neat. Jeff always wanted to sky dive but we never got around to it,
mabee some day. We did fly a paraglider, I built a tow rig that Jeff could let out the
string sending me higher and higher, his friend drove and he sat in the trailer with a
break handle in his hand, By the time we got to the end of the runway the string was
not fully extended so I told them the next time just turn around and come back and
I can get higher, this would have worked if my string didn't catch on a runway light,
I had to disconnect and fly down.

BUILT A CABIN

When I got out of the Air Force Jeff was about six months old so I took him with
me to build the cabin the woods in Arkansas, he stayed in his Johnny jump up most
of the time. While I was building, we lived in a tent, I washed him in creek water
warmed by the sun and washed diapers in a bucket, His mom was still in
the Air Force.

When Jeff was about two or three years old he fell out of the second story window onto the rocky cliff herebelow, I grabbed him up and hurried to the hospital, he wasn't breathing, after x-rays the doctor said that he was just fine, Thank God I was so worried.

All this time Jeff and I were going to church and serving the Lord, I believe that he enjoyed church and loved our pastor, we learned a lot together, one time we visited another church and Jeff was filled with The Holy Ghost and spoke with tongues as the Spirit gave utterance, I was so glad for him.

After he got out I went to visit him, it was so fun to be with him again, I got my son back. Now he is married to a fine woman and is in bible collage, he wants to be a youth pastor. I am so proud of him and so thankful to my god for his saving power.

GERRY

When I was about six years old we lived in Utah and my older brother Gerry would take me up a creek that we called Beaver Dam because there were so many beavers and dams along the creek. The pools of water backed up by the dams were filled with giant rainbow trout. Gerry would slowly wade through the water and scoop up a fish with his hands and toss it over to the bank where I was waiting to stop it from flopping back into the water, this was quite a challenge for a six year old, I had so much fun trying and only a few made it back into the water, I found that stomping on them usually worked. My mom's freezer was always full of fish. We would explore and catch snakes also. One time Gerry took me up there in the winter, my hands and feet got really cold, he tried to warm my feet by rubbing them with his hands, my dad was real mad at him. Gerry said that everyone that he brought up there got hurt some how.

 It was during this time that I came home from first grade in school and as I entered the front door I saw a milk dud, oh boy, I grabbed it and popped it in my mouth, it tasted terrible, it was a dingle berry that had just fallen out of my little brother's diaper. I guess that's why our moms tell us not to eat things you find on the ground.

When I was in third grade Gerry took me in the back yard and pulled out a joint, lit it and handed it to me and said breath it in deep, so I did, I would do just about anything he said. After that he gave me one to take to school almost every day, me and a friend named Dave would smoke it behind the school playground. Later when we moved to the rabbit farm Gerry made us two vodka and orange juices from my mom's cupboard, He didn't drink his so I drank both of them, I was so drunk that I tried to fly but after that I didn't feel good so Gerry tried to straiten me out before our parents got home, he made me drink three glasses of milk, before I could get up I vomited all over the kitchen table in front of the maid who told on us, Gerry was in trouble again.

I built a tree fort in the park by our house and I wanted to spend the night in it, at seven I was still afraid of the dark so I set out to put electricity in it, I spent all day digging two perfect holes in a piece of ¾ plywood and plugged in a lamp, it didn't work, I asked my dad why and he laughed.

Gerry didn't treat me very good but I had a lot of fun with him, he did things like through me in a trash can pouring beer on me while laughing at me with his friends. He sent me for my dad's beer and when I came back he and his buddy were covered in toothpaste, they said; help us. Most of these things happened in my fort, it was a converted doll house on the farm that I moved into at the age of twelve. One night Gerry had a girl friend in the fort, so I signaled Mike, lets leave, but we only left to peep through the small holes in the wall, that was our first experience in seeing any thing like that, just then Gerry saw us, we went running, we just knew he was going to kill us, then my mom came out and saved us.

When we didn't have anything to do we would get our dog stoned, he was trained to catch rabbits without hurting them but when both of them were stoned it was funny to watch.

We took my little brother's gumball machine, put a hole in one gumball and put in mescaline it was like L.S.D. or Acid, we put it back in the machine and gave John a penny to buy it, we waited for him to react but he didn't, we always that was very strange.

At the shack on the hill Gerry and I found a raccoon under the cupboard, we wanted to catch it so I ran to the house and grabbed a trash can, it was crazy trying to get that mean old raccoon into it, finally we got it and put him in a rabbit cage, we called him rocky raccoon, we fed him baby rabbits and watched how he would wash himself after eating.

Gerry had a spider monkey named Peppy, he was part of our family. Peppy would make our little dog so mad because he could not catch him. Peppy would jump down out of the tree in our front yard and steal a drink of my mom's bourbon, he liked getting stoned too. Peppy would ride around everywhere on Gerry's shoulder.

Gerry was a cook and he got me my first job washing dishes. One time in the fort we were board and had no drugs so Gerry put some napkins in a bag and squirted lighter fluid in it, we huffed and puffed until we were out of our minds, then Gerry said; let's burn the evidence, when he lit it the flames went everywhere and caught the fort on fire.

On the farm the sale of rabbits was not very profitable but the worms under the cages were gold, we just had to dig them out.

I had a stud pony named Thunder, He always tried to throw me off and he was good at it, we would be running really fast, get a whiff of mares and cut to the right leaving me in the dirt, one time he just stopped and I kept going landing in the dirt. When he threw me off he would always go to the shack on the hill leaving me miles away, we got him stoned too.

Gerry recently decided to serve the Lord and allowed me to baptize him. Thank God!

HOLY GHOST POWER

When I started going to church I didn't know about being baptized in the Holy Ghost, but I found in the bible that Jesus promised it and Paul wrote about it. "he shall baptize you with the Holy Ghost and power" " the place was shaken…and they were all filled with the Holy Ghost" "on the gentiles also was poured out the gift of the Holy Ghost for they heard them speak with tongues" "he that speaketh in an unknown tongue speaketh… unto God: for no man understand him; but in the spirit he speaks mysteries" "he that speaketh in an unknown tongue edifieth himself" (charge up his battery) Paul said; "I would that you all spoke with tongues" "let him that speaketh in an unknown tongue pray that he may interpret" "I thank my God, that I speak with tongues more than ye all" "Wherefore brethren, covet to prophecy, and forbid not to speak with tongues"

So while I was seeking this at church, I prayed and prayed every day that I would be filled, and on one night while I was praying some strange words came out of my mouth, right away I thought that this is not of God, but then thought; the Devil doesn't want me to praise God with tongues, so I continued. I felt very excited and charged up about serving the Lord, which is when I went door to door inviting people to church. One day I was at the alter everyone was praying, mostly in tongues, then I heard someone speak in tongues differently and louder, I knew it was a message, the church became silent, while my eyes were closed I saw words written above me. Was I supposed to give this interpretation? My heart was pounding heavily, I was afraid to speak these words, so I kept silent, just then someone behind me in a loud voice said the same words that I saw. How could this be? I felt very excited about it, but also felt that I should have spoken, so I promised the Lord that if he gave me another chance that I would not keep silent, and the Lord did give me many other opportunities to be used in the nine gifts of the Holy ghost. One time there was a visitor in our church, while everyone was praying he stood up and gave a prophecy "there is someone here that has a lump in her breast, and your tests show that it is cancer, but I tell you that the Lord has healed you this day" How could he have known, nobody knew in this church of about fifty. When this lady went to get another x-ray the tumor was gone!

SWIM TO AN ISLAND

One time when I was working in California, I saw an island just of the coast of San Clemente. I decided that I wanted to swim out there, so I set out, about half way I looked back, it was further than I thought, mabee I should go back, but I'm half way and I can rest when I get there. I kept on swimming, when I got there it was just a pile of jagged rocks and the waves crashing against them kept me from getting close, so I swam around to the back, I looked and found that it was about fifteen feet high strait up, I thought how did those sea lions get up there? In just that moment a sea lion floated up on a wave, well, I said; I can do that. The next wave came and I floated right up and I grabbed on, at that moment I realized that there was a sea lion with her pup and she was barking at me showing her long teeth, in that same moment the wave returned and took me with it. The sea lion jumped into the water, I knew she was after me. I was already thinking that mabee there is sharks out here but now an angry sea lion. I started swimming fast as I could, I finally got far enough away to not worry about the sea lion, so I stopped to rest and felt strong currents pulling and pushing me, so I kept swimming, not getting to rest on the island. I finally made it close to the shore when this huge wave crashed over me throwing me into the sand tumbling under the water, when I came up for a breath of air I had charley horses in both my legs and could not walk, just then another wave hit me, crashing into the shore. I just lay on the beach thanking God that I made it out. Thank you Jesus for helping me even when I do dumb things.

CASTLE CAVE IN

I was building a castle in Arkansas with big heavy rocks, after building the second floor I started bringing buckets of water, sand and rock up the stairs, to stage for work the next day, all together it was about three tons. I had worked so hard to get to this point in construction with the hope of making a lot of progress the next day. I was standing there after I finished looking at it when the whole floor caved in, I could have been buried under all that, I was scared at first, but I made it out OK, I started to get depressed because all that work was done in vain. Instead I prayed and some scriptures about the devil came to mind, I was angry with him, so I wrote a song about it. Burn devil burn.

BURN DEVIL BURN

Satan hindered me and he told me a lie, he came against me with all the powers of hell.   He hates me because I serve the Lord with all my heart, but I know his place is in the lake of fire. Burn devil burn forever. God shall bruise the head of Satan under your feet, I beheld Satan fall from heaven, the devils are subject to us in his name, behold I give you power over devils, I resist you devil so now flee from me, get thee behind me Satan and enter the swine, devil you believe in God, so now tremble, when you come in like a flood I will lift a standard against you. Devil if you bother me I'll read my bible more, if you tempt me I'll pray to the Lord all day, Lord lay hold on the devil and cast him in the pit, the liar thrown into the fire, Satan I hate you because you first hated me, I stand with my armor on to oppose you. The word of God in my heart is my weapon. Burn Devil Burn.

Some people like Roy may think that there is a DARK CLOUD over me because of the stories I tell, but every time that I am in the dark clouds of troubles I know that Jesus is with me, he will bring me out and make everything better than it was before the trouble started, that is why I can be happy in times of trouble and in the good times, he will do this for you if you ask him.

Exodus 20;21
Moses went into the dark cloud were God was....

Psalm 92;2
Dark clouds are around him.....

Printed in the United States
By Bookmasters